Kinship and Pilgrimage

Kinship and Pilgrimage

RITUALS OF REUNION IN AMERICAN PROTESTANT CULTURE

Gwen Kennedy Neville

New York   Oxford
OXFORD UNIVERSITY PRESS
1987

Oxford University Press

Oxford   New York   Toronto
Delhi   Bombay   Calcutta   Madras   Karachi
Petaling Jaya   Singapore   Hong Kong   Tokyo
Nairobi   Dar es Salaam   Cape Town
Melbourne   Auckland
and associated companies in
Beirut   Berlin   Ibadan   Nicosia

Copyright © 1987 by Gwen Kennedy Neville
First printed as an Oxford University Press paperback 2005
Published by Oxford University Press, Inc.,
200 Madison Avenue, New York, New York 10016

Oxford is a registered trademark of Oxford University Press

Library of Congress Cataloging-in-Publication Data
Neville, Gwen Kennedy, 1938–
Kinship and pilgrimage.
Bibliography: p.   Includes index.
1. Reunions—Religious aspects—Christianity.
2. Reunions—United States.   3. Christian pilgrims
and pilgrimages.   I. Title.
BR517.N.48   1987   306'.6   86-12746
ISBN 0-19-504338-3; 0-19-530033-5 (pbk)

1 2 3 4 5 6 7 8 9 10
Printed in the United States of America
on acid-free paper

Acknowledgments

Many people participated in the creation of this book and in the research on which it is based. Those who welcomed me into their communities as I conducted my ethnographic work are at the top of the list of those to whom I am grateful: the people of Montreat, North Carolina; the participants in numerous reunions and kin-religious gatherings across the Southeastern United States; and the residents of the Scottish towns where I lived and worked. I especially thank the individuals who submitted to lengthy interviews and those who assisted me in finding special documents and local histories. In addition, I appreciate the assistance of my students who, over the years, have listened to my lectures, challenged me with questions, and studied their own family gatherings and religious traditions as a part of class projects.

Funding of my ethnographic fieldwork was provided in part by the National Endowment for the Humanities; the Graduate Fellowship Program at the University of Florida; the Emory University Reseach Council; the Cullen Faculty Development Fund of Southwestern University; and The Brown Foundation, Inc., of Houston, through its support of activities associated with the Elizabeth Root Paden Chair in Sociology at Southwestern University.

As this manuscript evolved numerous individuals discussed my ideas with me, read segments of the work, and made suggestions. It would be impossible to thank all of them, but they include Conrad Arensberg, James Boon, Walt Herbert, Barbara Meyerhoff, Alexander Moore, James Peacock, Christopher Smout, and Victor Turner. Advisors in the early phases of my research included Carol Taylor, Elizabeth Eddy, and Solon Kimball. Kimball served as director of my dissertation on Montreat and was a skillful, sympathetic teacher and a good friend. I thank Dotty Secor for typing this manuscript; the editors at Oxford University Press who followed it through to publication; and, finally, the numerous friends, both in and out of academia, who encouraged and supported me during the years of this project.

My deepest gratitude is to my colleague and co-fieldworker, my husband Jack Hunnicutt, and to Katherine, Mary Grace, and Ken. To these four people this book is dedicated.

Georgetown, Texas   G. K. N.
February 1986

Contents

Kinship and Pilgrimage

Introduction

THE TWIN THREADS of kinship and pilgrimage run deep in the fabric of Protestant culture. Kinship, on the one hand, is a concept calling on all the reverences for family membership, parent-child relationships, honoring thy father and mother, belonging to a group of relatives who help one another and love one another, belonging to a closely knit community. Pilgrimage, on the other hand, summarizes the process of leaving home to seek one's fortune that forms the complementary side of Anglo-American Protestant life. One must leave the warm, loving relationship of family and kin in order to fulfill the obligation of becoming an individual, acting out one's destiny, being actualized as a self. These notions of family membership versus individual identity, of belonging versus breaking loose to succeed alone, form powerful motifs in Western literature, art, and religious writing. In plays, in films, in television dramas, in serious psychoanalytic works and psychological studies, as well as in the popular psychological analyses of magazines and advice columnists, in social science studies of community, individual, and society—in all these one finds repeated the antithetical ideals of being a part of a family and being an individual alone. These powerful themes are also expressed in social form. One of the most visible outcroppings of the generally subterranean configuration is in the complex of gatherings in the Southern United States known as *reunions*.

Reunions are assemblies of kin and cobelievers in a religious tradition who have been scattered by the processes of urbanization and industrialization. These rituals occur in a pattern of cyclical regularity at rural churches, cemeteries, camp meeting grounds, old home places, and religious conference centers. They are held in honor of founding members who came to this country or who were pioneers in newly opened geographical and ideological territories. They assemble people who define themselves as belonging to a large group descended from one or more of these ancestors. They honor the living family and the dead, they include religious activities as well as kin-based ones. I have called the gatherings *kin-religious gatherings*, and I have discovered in them a complicated symbolic statement of cultural themes that lies at the heart of the Protestant belief system and the Protestant way of life. The gatherings, in fact, form a pilgrimage system based on the reverse of the medieval and Roman Catholic pilgrimage that has been more fully described and studied. The Protestant pilgrimage system of *returning home* from wandering out forms a complement to the Roman Catholic system of *traveling outward* from home on a pilgrim journey in order to seek one's spiritual "fortune" in the form of salvation or expiation.

In analyzing these gatherings I combine the study of social process with the study of cultural expression, following in the tradition of symbolic anthropology and processual analysis. As social process the events I have detailed provide a web of friendship and kinship that links together wide networks of people who otherwise live in scattered nuclear families in urban settings. The gatherings also provide a repeated set of communal rituals for the cyclical resocialization of the participants and for the recruitment of the new generations of children into the culture. In addition to serving these social functions, which are fairly obvious to the even partially trained observer, the gatherings are significant *cultural* entities. When I use the term *culture*, I do not refer to the inventory of quaint folkways or old-world traditions that may be maintained by assemblies of this type, for to speak of culture in this way is to remain within an analysis of social function and limit one's insight to the purely pragmatic nature of human symbolic creativity. I use culture to refer to the complex of meanings and symbols that gives to human social life a framework. In other words, I treat culture as separate from, but certainly not removed from, behavior. In fact, I attempt to combine these two entities or concepts into a holistic view for observing, and perhaps partially understanding, culture as it is expressed in human behavioral terms (Turner and Turner 1978:xiv).

In using this approach to the study of Roman Catholic pilgrimage, Victor and Edith Turner explain their analytical devices and point of view as follows.

> Not that we consider the ideas, norms, values, symbols, and other constructs, which constitute the "coherent system of symbols and meanings" (Schneider 1968:8) of Catholic pilgrimage to be fully independent of pilgrim behaivor. Rather do we regard such "cultural units" (to use Schneider's term) as "expressed in" (see Hanson 1975:102) actual pilgrim behavior. Thus we find that the doctrine of the Assumption of the Blessed Virgin Mary, for example, is intrinsically involved with several concrete aspects of Marian pilgrimage. . . .
>
> (Turner and Turner 1978:xiv)

Protestant pilgrimage as I have understood and presented it is in this same way a concrete social reality expressing cultural themes within the Protestant system of symbols and meanings. When Protestant reunion rituals are seen as pilgrimage and as cultural expression, this intricate set of phenomena become the observable form in which elusive cultural realities are articulated and through which they are discoverable. In adopting this method of analysis and this theoretical perspective, one asks not only "What function do these reunions serve for the Protestant individual and for the society?", but also "What does this behavior or cluster of behaviors *mean?*" Schneider states the posture for investigation as follows.

> The study of culture is concerned, then, with the study of social action as a *meaningful* system of action, and is therefore, by definition, concerned with the question of "meaning-in-action".
>
> (Schneider 1976:199)

My own investigation has been colored by these definitions as well as by those of Geertz (1973), who sees culture as a text rather than as an organism or a machine, the favorite analogies of the social anthropologists of an earlier time. The dramatic and narrative models of Peacock (1968) have shed new light on my own data and its subsequent interpretation. My understanding of the concept of culture has been enriched by the ideas of James Boon (1973; 1982) and of Milton Singer (1984). I have followed closely the symbolic analysis of Victor and Edith Turner, whose anthropological study of pilgrimage has made an important intellectual contribution to my own models and analyses (Turner 1969; Turner and Turner 1978). In addition to these scholars whose cultural understandings provide the theoretical foundation for this analysis, Conrad Arensberg and Solon T. Kimball (1965) have contributed to my understanding of human community as social process and as an expression of culture. Calling on the theory and method of social anthropology, especially that of Lloyd Warner (1961), Arensberg and Kimball describe and explain the nature of symbolic action, as expressed in the cultural patterning of time, space, seasons, and cycles, in the arrangements of persons in a particular social space, and in the structure of social action and social relationships. When reread in the light of symbolic anthropology and interpretation theory, their statements about the community as ordered social action patterned by cultural codes seem surprisingly current.

I began my research in 1970 with an ethnographic study of a Presbyterian summer community, Montreat, North Carolina, where devout Protestants had assembled every summer since the turn of the century to hold religious conferences, vacation, and visit with kin. My awe at discovering intricate patterns and processes in the ritual life and the elaborate emphasis on kinship of this community—a temporary community of people who lived in scattered nuclear families throughout the secular society—led me to ask new questions about kinship and religion in Protestant America. It led me to a series of studies done between 1970 and 1985 that focused on Protestant religious and kin-based ritual life. Over the years these studies have included family reunions, church homecomings, anniversaries, decoration days, cemetery association days, and camp meetings in North Carolina, Georgia, and Texas in the United States and outdoor preachings and church anniversaries in the south of Scotland.[1] In addition to participant observation—that tried and true basic technique of the cultural anthropologist—I have used ethnographers' various tools for charting, counting, and mapping behavior and social arrangements and for noting and tracking the symbols and processes of ritual. I also interviewed individuals who had attended many gatherings over a long period of time and asked certain people to write about their experiences or to solicit written descriptions of gatherings from their own families. I spent many hours in university and town libraries in the United States and Scotland reading about past and present gatherings in my effort to understand just what was going on and to place whatever it was in the broadest ethnological context. I have presented my findings and my analyses as a series of ethnographies surrounded by several chapters of ethnological framing. I have attempted to do what Geertz (1973) calls "thick description" in order to describe behavior and simultaneously communicate information about symbols, meanings, and codes that can be discovered through the careful interpretation of concrete behaviors and their symbolic representations.

My ethnographies of the Southern family and church gatherings are intended to be representative of phenomena pervasive in the region, yet they are not exhaustive in presenting information or description on all subregions, denominations, or social strata of the Southern United States. Variations occur, to be sure, based on subregion and on the social class and denomination of the participants. It is also true that there exist in the cities and elite suburbs of the American South great numbers of Southerners who would find these gatherings quite foreign and who might even be offended to be included in what they resist as a stereotype of Southern backwardness and rurality. If these individuals do attend a reunion of the greater family it may be held at a country club or hotel, and be catered. Even the variations, however, will conform to certain accepted cultural rules and contain certain fixed features that will be found in all the events. The point of my ethnographic presentations is not to present survey data on statistical occurrence but, instead, to describe and analyze a particular set of social *forms*. These forms will be congruent with events known to Southerners and to other Protestant Americans who have roots in the shared tradition. My aim is to create a picture of each of these events and then to provide a framework for analysis and comparison. The test of accuracy for the ethnographies is whether Protestants who have attended such gatherings can read and clearly recognize the activities in which they themselves have participated and then understand them in a new way. The test of accuracy for the analytical models is whether these models have the power to explain other aspects of Protestant culture in comparison to Catholic culture and to make them more intelligible ethnologically.

In presenting my models and my data I give first the broad outline of pilgrimage as a social and a cultural phenomenon, and I discuss in detail why I consider these particular Protestant assemblies as a pilgrimage complex. Chapter Two deals with the history and structure of open-air services. In Chapters Three to Five I tell the story of three different kinds of gatherings. The first gathering is the family reunion of the American South. Gatherings of this type are not celebrated in Scotland, nor is there a record of such gatherings in the history of the Scottish Presbyterians. The family reunion is apparently a product of the colonizing migrations, which created a world of social and geographic mobility and gave to its participants a complicated set of cultural prescriptions and contradictions. Chapter Three, the second ethnographic chapter, focuses on three variations on the sacred place as expressions of the outdoor church: the cemetery reunion, the church homecoming, and the camp meeting. These all embody certain themes of the covenanting tradition, or the open-air communions of the nineteenth century, and express a style and shape of liturgical form that is in its essence antihierarchical and antiestablishmentarian. Each gathering is an assemblage of interconnected sets of families, producing a larger version of the family reunion, now based on a sacred place instead of on common descent. The final type of Protestant pilgrimage I discuss is that of the denominational conference center, which is the most complicated and most elaborate expression of the complex of gatherings. For each denomination, it is the central pilgrim shrine. In this case the conference cummunity described and analyzed is that of Montreat, North Carolina, spiritual home of the Presbyterians in the South. Similar Methodists or Baptist centers could be described, each stating its own meanings through its own particular symbolic code—the cultural "dialect" within the ritual language of Anglo-Saxon Protestantism. Chapter Six summarizes these ethnographic materials and places the descriptions in theoretical perspective.

I do not attempt here to prove a one-to-one correspondence between a social institution and a cultural system; such a tight correspondence is impossible to identify and delineate. This task would be impossible because, as Schneider has pointed out, "institutions" in the social, functional sense are not isomorphic with what he calls cultural "galaxies"—configurations of symbols and meanings. Cultural "galaxies" are "not limited to one institutional system but spread far beyond its boundaries" (Schneider 1976:210). My attempt is to define and describe in the "thickest" possible way one particular instance of the intersection of a cultural system of meanings with an observable social expression. It is an attempt to demonstrate how culture is expressed in and through human ceremonial life, in this case, how the meanings of Reformed Protestant theology and belief are related to the concrete aspects of Protestant kinship and religious gatherings. In addition, it is an attempt to place this system of interconnected symbolic expressions into its broad cultural-historical position as the expression of a meaning system for the Protestant world that stands as a dramatic contrast to and in many ways is a *reversal*, or an *inversion*, of the meaning system of the Roman Catholic universe.

I have chosen to deal with the outdoor gatherings as types of events expressing cultural statements through symbolic processes, but they could, of course, be viewed from other perspectives, such as religious, historical, or sociological. In the writings of various historians and sociologists the family reunion and the camp meeting have both been seen in these alternate ways. My own treatment follows in the footsteps of cultural anthropologists studying nonindustrial societies. Each event is treated as a symbolic form in which people have expressed their cultural meanings and their values over time and space. Historians will wish for more detailed treatment of specific contexts; scholars of religion will wish for a closer tie to theological trends and religious ideologies; and perhaps the sociologists will wish for more quantitative data and some attempt at hypothesis testing. I have touched on each of these various other fields and borrowed from them in an attempt to place my ethnographic data into a holistic framework; however, my work remains essentially—and unapologetically—cultural anthropology.

PART ONE

Pilgrimage

CHAPTER ONE

Pilgrimage as Social Process in Roman Catholic and Protestant Culture

IN THE STRICT sense pilgrimage does not exist in Protestant society or culture. One of the "abuses" renounced by the Reformers at the time of the Protestant Reformation was that of pilgrimage, which was said to support the theology of salvation by works, one that the Protestant theologians deplored. If one looks more closely, however, at how Protestant individuals and families move across the landscape of the Southern United States and the south of Scotland—both strongholds of Reformed Christianity—one finds that a pattern of travel to sacred places in honor of revered saints and ancestors does exist. This is, after all, the classical Oxford English Dictionary definition of a pilgrim: "one who journeys to a sacred place as an act of religious devotion." Yet in Protestant culture these journeys are not so defined; they are certainly not called pilgrimages by their devout participants. I intend to explore in this chapter why this is true. Pilgrimage does, in fact, exist in Protestantism, and it is an important symbolic statement for its adherents.[1]

The pilgrimage centers to which I refer in the travel pattern of devout Protestants are connected not with a salvation by works or with the propitiation of saints or intercessors, but with a salvation based on faith alone, accompanied by good works because of the person's having been saved by the grace of God. The centers are associated not with miracles or visions of saints, but with historical narratives of hardworking, God-fearing folk who settled a wilderness, opposed a king or an established church tradition, or raised a large family "in the nurture and admonition of the Lord." The centers are rural churches, church or family cemeteries, family homeplaces, camp meeting grounds, open fields near ruined churches, or markers of famous battles. They are hallowed by everyday people who lived godly lives and therefore demonstrated their participation in the Communion of Saints, to which the living members and all their descendants also belong. These culturally defined features are strikingly different from those of Roman Catholic pilgrimage; they create a very different reality for Protestants. Yet pilgrimage in each of these different cultural worlds can be seen as social processes sharing certain structural characteristics.[2]

The social processual aspects of pilgrimage, along with its cultural properties, have been studied extensively by Turner and Turner (1978), who identify pilgrimage as an example of institutionalized antistructure, a liminality that exists over, against, and apart from the ordered, structured social world of the city and town in the medieval period and in contemporary Roman Catholic Europe and Mexico. This liminal aspect of pilgrimage can be seen both in medieval society and in the mobile, urban, primarily Protestant society of today. Each culture—the Roman Catholic and the Protestant—creates its own version of the liminoid phenomenon of pilgrimage; each style of pilgrimage provides what Geertz (1973) would call a "metasocial commentary" on its own social universe. And one—the Protestant pilgrim complex—is a symbolic inversion of the other—that of Roman Catholicism.

In their study of Roman Catholic pilgrimage in the Western world the Turners state that they have attempted "to expound the interrelations of symbols and meanings framing and motivating pilgrim behavior in a major world religion" "to map and frame some of the institutional 'territories' within which pilgrimage processes circulate, and to suggest how institutional changes within pilgrimage may be linked to changes outside it" (Turner and Turner 1978:xiv-xv). They combine anthropological and historical methods in the attempt to uncover the underlying cultural and social processes associated with classical pilgrimage and to see these ritual systems in their overall context.

Medieval pilgrimages are seen in the Turners' study within the construct of ritual *liminality* as defined by van Gennep (1909). The pilgrim in medieval Christianity was a person in transition, entering on a long journey to a saint's shrine in order to experience penance or expiation or to fulfill a vow to a departed loved one. By the visit to the saint's shrine the pilgrim was transformed from his or her daily state of structured social requirements and personal village obligations into a new state of communal life shared with the other pilgrims. Through his or her pilgrimage the person underwent a process similar to a tribal initiation, becoming removed from society in order to become purified and immersed in the sacred lore and then being returned in a renewed state, one of greater spirituality. Turner finds no place in early Roman Christianity other than the monastery and the pilgrimage where this type of process occurs. The pilgrimage, then, was the only way for a layperson to enter fully into the ritual condition that Turner labels *liminoid.* By undertaking a pilgrimage an individual in feudal and semifeudal Europe became intentionally separated from the tight world of the medieval burgh or village—possibly lessening his or her chances for individual gain in power or status because of the long absence and expending large amounts of money to pay for the expenses of the journey—and entered into a particular style of life suited to the *pilgrim way.* Thousands entered on this path each year to the various shrines throughout Europe and Britain, and the institutionalization of this tradition gave rise to a body of myth, folklore, and literature all its own.

The Medieval Pilgrimage

The central feature of these pilgrimages, described extensively in studies of the Middle Ages,[3] is that they are directed toward a specific sacred place sanctified by (1) an incident in the life of Jesus, (2) the corpse of a saint or a saint's relic, or (3) a visitation or a vision of a particular saint or martyr.[4] Once the focal point of the pilgrimage had been established along one of these themes, its sanctity was increased by the number of pilgrims who came to its door; the more pilgrims who visited and reported on a shrine, the greater its attraction became for future hordes. Each shrine was in the custody of a monastic house, and the various orders of monks grew in wealth, power, and political importance as various shrines grew in popularity. Cathedrals were often associated in medieval times with relics, saints, and pilgrims, and in this way certain bishoprics maintained their power. The monastic houses were responsible for the roads and bridges that led to their shrines and for lodging and feeding the pilgrims. Hall (1965) links pilgrimages, in fact, directly to the rise and fall of monasticism, since the monks were dependent for their financial support on the system of offerings and gifts that resulted both from money given at the shrines and money exchanged in return for services. An additional economic effect of pilgrimage centers was the growth of fairs and markets in conjunction with important saints' days and religious calendrical festivals. A number of towns in England owe their origins to the stalls and stands erected in a line leading up the road to the cathedral. The growth of fairs, markets, and revelry associated with pilgrimages was one of the reasons given by the reformers of a later day that pilgrimages should be abolished.

The settlement pattern of medieval Northern Europe and Britain was one of feudal domains dotted with manorial villages and scattered burghs, commercial towns chartered by the king or given in fealty to a lord or an abbey. The literature of the period suggests an intervillage and interburgh movement that belies the image of quiet, localized, parochial life.

Among the royalty and aristocracy, movement was a regular feature of life, with the entire entourage of the king relocating periodically in the homes of nobles on a rotating basis as an economic necessity to support the huge cluster of people in their courtly life-style. Movement of ordinary people between villages and towns was based on commercial ventures or religious motivations. In his study of English wayfaring life of the period, Jusserand (1950) lists a catalog of travelers including merchants, peddlers, messengers, wandering workmen, peasants out of bond, outlaws, herbalists, charlatans, minstrels, and jugglers and tumblers in addition to the wandering preachers and friars and ever-present pilgrims. Underlying the travel pattern was the basic premise that each ordinary citizen was rooted in a particular village or town within a highly structured set of social relationships based on class, kinship, and inherited position in the collage of trade guilds, working jobs, and franchised mercantile privileges. The professional travelers (peddlers, wandering workmen, minstrels, etc.) were in their role because of an inherited place in society and would be seen as outcasts or as marginals in every village. The village or town resident who wished to "see the world" was provided with a socially acceptable format for temporary exploration in the institution of pilgrimage; he or she could enter into the *communitas* of the pilgrim journey and visit to the shrine as a way of escaping, for a time, from the pressing obligations of the structure within which all of routine daily life was necessarily enacted.

The process of undergoing a pilgrimage was at once a separation from the village or burgh and an indentification with the sacred meanings and symbols that comprised the Christian life to the pre-Reformation Christian. This view of life, according to the Turners' analysis, conceived of the individuals in a lifelong drama, a struggle for salvation, in which the person is never quite sure of his or her salvation but is constantly in interaction with a cast of characters who alternately assist and tempt away the solitary soul. The actors in the drama include, in Turner's words,

> some visible, some invisible, some natural, some supernatural: God; Mary, Mother of God; the angels; the saints; and the three divisions of the living church, the Church Triumphant of the invisible souls in heaven; the Church Suffering of the invisible souls in purgatory; and the Church Militant of living mortals beleagured in the world by flesh and the devil, and by human adversaries. The individual soul is seen as dramatically involved, until the moment of death with all these persons, personages, and corporate groups.   (Turner and Turner 1978:15)

Through undertaking a pilgrimage, the person increased his or her chances for salvation. Because souls might help one another through the drama of life, a primary motive for going on pilgrimage was to put oneself in touch with some of the most effective helpers, especially the saints in heaven, accessible through a particular saint's shrine. The act of pilgrimage itself was regarded as a "good work" and would increase the person's chances of salvation.

At the pilgrim shrine a whole complex of symbolic materials drew the pilgrim into an attitude of reverence. The buildings themselves, many of which were impressive cathedrals or other monumental structures, the iconography, and even the landmarks leading up to the shrine were made sacred both by their own communicative, evocative power and by the legacy of sacred tales and legends that had grown up around each one. These shrines provide a classic example of the concrete social expression of what Turner calls *root paradigms*—"cultural models for behavior that exist in the heads of the main actors in a social drama, whether in a small group or on the stage of history" (Turner 1974:64).

In Roman Catholic Christianity, the root paradigms derive from certain key pronouncements of Jesus and his immediate followers, the apostles, as well as other holy lives and works of the founders of the religion. Mary, the Mother of Jesus, also has a prominent role. The saints' shrines, in their symbolic expressions of the paradigms at the root of the Roman Catholic cultural world, present dramatic images drawn from the founder's life, especially the crises of birth, coming of age, and death. Thus, at the shrines we invariably see "images, icons, and paintings of Jesus as infant, child, young preacher, scourged victim, crucified scapegoat, and resurrected God-man" (Turner and Turner 1978:10).

The concept of root paradigm as used by Victor Turner is very close to the concept of *root metaphor* used by Stephen Pepper (1942:91), to whom Turner refers, and also close to the notion of *conceptual archetype* used by Max Black (1962:240). Pepper's term, root metaphor, was adopted by Turner in some of his earlier work and is sometimes attributed to him by students of symbolic anthropology. What Pepper was talking about when he said "root metaphor" was, according to Black, "how metaphysical systems ('world hypotheses,' as he calls them) arise; but his remarks have wider application" (Black 1962:240). In the application of each of these labels, a theorist—a philospher, linguist, or social anthropologist—is trying to specify a process of symbolization that goes beyond the ordinary understanding of symbol. In this basic symbolic process in the conceptualization of reality, a culture constructs clusters of meanings, and these meanings then are framed into what Black called a "systematic repertoire of ideas" (1962:241). This repertoire provides a pool from which to draw analogical extensions about the nature of the universe and of day-to-day events—a pool that is available to the writer, poet, and artist of a given time period or cultural milieu and also to the ordinary person on the street and to the pilgrim engaged in the act of devotion.

The Roman Catholic pilgrimage makes certain metaphorical statements about the Roman Catholic universe. The foundation metaphors of preindustrial European Christianity and society are clearly seen in classical pilgrimage. Nisbet (1969) has utilized the notion of foundation metaphor in viewing broad conceptualizations of various societies about the nature of things and of the universe and has, in fact, suggested that social change is intricately bound up in the process of changing world view and the consequent change in symbolic statements. Nisbet is quoted as commenting that what we usually call revolutions in thought are "quite often no more than the mutational replacement, at certain critical points in history, of one foundation metaphor by another in man's contemplation of universe, society, and self" (Nisbet 1969:6, quoted in Turner 1974:28).

The revolution in thought that has attended the Protestant Reformation has indeed been radical. In the upheavals of social and economic life that preceded and accompanied the industrial period in European history, the root paradigms of Roman Catholic Christianity can also be seen to have been upended. It is not surprising that the emergent liminal social process of the Protestant pilgrimage should represent a symbolic inversion of these root paradigms and give social expression to the culture of a new world.

Protestantism and Pilgrimage

The Protestant Reformation brought an end to the institutionalized pilgrimage. Reformers in England and Scotland outlawed the saints' shrines and destroyed their relics. Pilgrimages were associated with the complex of ecclesiastical "abuses" that were abhorrent to leaders of the Reformation. In the writings of the period pilgrimages are denounced as being bound up with a salvation based on good works and on vows fulfilled instead of a salvation based on faith and on the grace of God. To the devout, reformed Christian, the individual's entire life became a pilgrimage process, a journey from birth to death walking in obedience to the laws of God. Undertaking a pilgrimage to a sacred shrine as part of working out one's salvation was unnecessary and blasphemous.

The social scientist looking at this period of radical theological change also perceives accompanying radical changes in economy, land use, and settlement pattern. The commercial and industrial economic complex was emerging, the cities and large towns drawing individuals away from the villages and burghs into the individuation of the factory-based economy. The tight-knit structures of medieval burgh and village life in the English Midlands gave way to the mobility of the workers in response to the jobs. The Highland Clearances in Scotland scattered thousands of clansfolk to the corners of the colonial empire to make room for commercial enterprises of sheep farming; in the Scottish Borders the early textile mills drew country people into the towns to swell town populations into double and triple their former size. The lure of the colonies drew hundreds of thousands from their villages and countryside to attempt new ventures in the Americas.

Over the 300 years of post-Reformation industrialism and the spread of Protestant Christians outward into the Americas, the Protestant version of the pilgrimage has taken shape. Its cultural prescriptions represent a reversal of the themes that predominate in medieval Christianity and subsequent Roman Catholicism. The ordinary person is now seen not as a resident of a parish or manorial domain over which the church holds sway and out of which he or she must travel in order to undertake a pilgrim journey, but as an individual citizen of the world at large on a personal pilgrimage through life and society. The emphasis on upward and outward mobility makes it necessary for persons not to view themselves as tied irrevocably to kinship or localized structures but as individuals free to "seek their fortunes," encountering as they go the difficulties and temptations that might once have been expected by the medieval pilgrim on the journey to Canterbury.

In the context of these reversals, the Protestant pilgrimage becomes one in which individualized new urban residents move periodically away from their industrial urban universe and back into the universe associated with the tight-knit kin groups of rural past semifeudal times.

The actual repeated journey made by the Protestant pilgrim is not one of going *out* as in the classical pilgrimage but one of going *back* periodically as a way of escaping the individuation and depersonalization experienced as a member of a scattered, mobile, and often anonymous urban industrial society. The journey is a sacred

one to a sacred place, made holy not by martyrs or saints but by a
community of believers over time.

At the same time that the social shape and style of "journey to
a sacred place" shifted, so did the complex of cultural meanings
associated with God and salvation. The root paradigms of the
Reformation Protestant tradition are antithetical to those of Roman
Catholicism, in which the soul engaged in a lifelong drama of
struggle for salvation. According to Calvinistic theology, the significant drama of salvation has already been played out in the
activity of God through Jesus Christ, who came to save the world
once and for all and in whom those who believe will be saved.
There is no struggle for the individual person to accumulate "good
works," because he or she has been saved already by grace and
justified through faith. The universe of the Christian life, then, is
populated not by an extensive cast of characters from the supernat-
ural world but only by God, Jesus Christ, and humanity. God
speaks his Word (a label for the activity of God, the written record
of this activity in the Bible, and the person of Jesus as savior)
directly to humanity, not through any intermediaries. The target of
God's revealing Word is, according to classical Reformed Christianity, the people who then form the "Community of the Saints,"
the "Covenant People," or "The People of God." The emphasis,
in other words, is not only on the lonely struggle of the individual
soul with the powers of evil as in Catholic tradition, but also it is on
the hearing and doing of the Word in a community of people, a
congregation. The congregation in Protestant life is not necessarily
the community of a person's origin; in fact, it rarely is. Nor does it
coincide with the kinship group; indeed, it is a spiritual community,
an ideational community, a community of faith that might, and
often does, require an individual to be different from or separate
from his or her own family of origin. It is formed by individuals
who have *moved* from local bonds in order to follow the individualistic imperative. It is nonhierarchical in its social form because the
cultural world for which it stands is a nonhierarchical one, truly an
antistructure to the structured, hierarchical world of the feudal
society and the medieval Church. The medieval pilgrimage is a
symbolic process commenting on the cultural contradictions implicit in a world in which the person lives within a tightly ordered,
traditional social system but is under the religious imperative to be

saved as an individual soul. The Protestant pilgrimage comments on the opposite—a world in which the person lives in a constant state of individual striving and self-actualization but in which the religious imperative calls for communal life and loyalty to one's family and kin. Both these worlds hold irreconcilable cultural contradictions. And, in each one, the pilgrimage acts as a vehicle for constructing meanings, for making sense of the contradictions, for attempting a ritual resolution of seemingly impossible cultural demands.

Another contrast of Roman Catholic to Protestant pilgrimage is that while Roman Catholic pilgrim shrines have sometimes led to the centralization of a population and to the growth of towns or cities, this is not the case for the seasonal sacred places of the Protestants. Turner points out that over time it is not uncommon for a Roman Catholic pilgrim shrine to become more and more secularized and overlaid with economic importance so that new miracles and new visions on the periphery of that population center may be generated and lead to the establishment of new pilgrim shrines on the margin of or in the rural areas (Turner 1974:227). In Protestant pilgrimage, meanwhile, the place itself has taken on a sacredness by repeated use over the years by a community of gathered believers. The miracles are couched in the language of individual conversion and changed lives of participants; the communitas is stated in the language of "fellowship"; and the economic load carried by the gathering of people is spread out into the hometowns and cities of the assembled because they have bought their supplies at home and come fully prepared for camping out or for holding a dinner on the grounds.

The pilgrimage that I am about to describe is not simply a subtype of Christian pilgrimage but an antitype, or an inversion of a previous and continuing type. It is Protestant pilgrimage expressing Protestant culture, an ordered and recurring symbolization in social form of the metaphors at the foundation of the Protestant world and of the contradictions implicit in that world.

The cultural themes of the Protestant tradition are woven into all three categories of Protestant pilgrimage. These include the themes of individuals leaving home for lands far away, establishing in the wilderness home sites, families, churches and, eventually, an Anglo-Saxon civilization; themes of brave and courageous defenders of the faith doing battle with the forces of evil in the world for the glory of God; and themes of a covenant community being established where the wickedness of the cities and the towns can be shut out. There are also more subtle, underlying kinds of messages communicated by the gatherings that do not find their way into the spoken tradition of sermons and speeches in the way those do that I have mentioned previously. The more subtle messages are those encoded in the body of social form and the symbolic use of time, space, and human groupings that preach in what Hall (1966) calls the "silent language" of cultural transmission. These messages have to do with the continuity of "sacred place," a tradition of rootedness in an otherwise rootless society; the placing of the human family in relation to God, who requires individual obedience; with the arrangement of that family into a continuing entity and its preservation in the face of mobility and dispersal; and with the separate cultural universes of female and male and the place of both in the meaning system associated with church and family. For a brief description to introduce the main features of the gatherings I have analyzed as pilgrimages, I have separated the gatherings into those that enshrine the extended family as a kinship entity, those that enshrine a sacred place, and those that enshrine the ideational community institutionalized as a religious conference center.

The Family and Kin

The first general type I have used as a vehicle for classifying these various kinship and religious-based assemblies into some form of order is that in which the primary focus is on the family itself, a gathering that enshrines and sacralizes the human family and connects it to the family of faith. The family reunion in the American South can take the shape of a large, extended family of hundreds of descendants honoring an ancestor who entered this country from Scotland or England, or it can be only a small cluster of the children and grandchildren of a colonizing or pioneering couple. The reunion may be held at an old family homeplace in the countryside, at a community hall or a hall in a state park, at a camp meeting ground, or at some other recurrent spot that has found its way into the traditional use of that particular family. In the activities of the reunion and in its use of time, space, and persons in various familial and practical roles, in its ceremonial use of food, and in its concern with the ancestors, the reunion constructs an image of the family as a cohesive, loving, and caring group in which the individual is subsumed and protected, if only temporarily, from the realities of his or her fragile nuclear family of day-to-day routines. The reunion family as a social group is a "cognatic descent group" in contrast to the bilateral kindred of mainstream secular America. It is also a symbolic enactment of the cultural constructs associated with the family of faith and with the contradiction implicit in a world that requires a person to separate from the human family in order to fulfill his or her individual destiny.

Sacred Place

The pilgrimage to the sacred place is often directed toward a rural church in the countryside where one's ancestors were among the founders and where those ancestors are at rest in the adjoining graveyard. For the gathering, known as a church homecoming or a church reunion, hundreds of former residents and the children and grandchildren of those residents will assemble annually on a Sunday to attend the morning worship services and take part in a communal meal known as "dinner on the grounds." Often associated with the homecoming is a day of cleaning the graveyard and decorating the graves with flowers. These gatherings take place in the American South (and I have learned of similar gatherings in the Midwest and other regions) and also, with regularity, in the South and Southwest of Scotland, where many of the American founding ancestors originated. In both these geographic locales, return to a sacred place for the homecoming—in Scotland and in some American locations known as the "anniversary"—constitutes a sacred journey for a special religious and family-related occasion.[5] The worship service that is shared embodies prayers and preaching directed toward the reverence for an honored local tradition. The outdoor meal afterward symbolizes the participation together in the true communion of fellowship and day-to-day sainthood that symbolically contrasts with the sharing of the indoor meal of the Eucharist, symbolically a part of the hierarchical and liturgical tradition of the Established Church world.

Gatherings based on sacred place also encompass the permanent locales known in the Southern United States as camp meeting grounds and the sacred places for field preachings and Conventicles in Scotland. All these gatherings—homecomings, camp meetings, and outdoor preachings—typify an outdoor tradition that includes a reverence for nature, sacred spots, and ancestors. Religious services are held in conjunction with family gatherings. The camp meeting as a gathering type has often been associated with the American frontier, especially the frontier of Kentucky and Tennessee during the days of revivalism among the Calvinists and Methodists in the early nineteenth century.[6] This event is also an expression of a deeply rooted cultural tradition shared by Anglo-Saxon frontier folk with other Saxon and Celtic peoples, a tradition I have described in Chapter Four. Frontier camp meetings were usually revivalist and evangelical in nature; contemporary camp meeting assemblies at the permanent camp meeting grounds in Georgia, North Carolina, and East Tennessee (some of which were begun in this earlier revival style) are presently attended by a recurring group of families who own cabins and return year after year—a temporary expression of the ongoing "people of God" in the same fashion that the homecoming and the anniversary at churches symbolize in social form this elusive theological goal.

The Religious Summer Community

The third and final type of gathering I present here is the ideational community, embodying the "intentional communitas" of Turner (1969). This type includes the religious conferences, retreat centers, and denominational summer communities that dot the landscape of the mountains of Western North Carolina and are, in fact, found in a variety of recreational rural settings at lakes, hills, and seasides throughout America. In these locations there are frequently permanent cottages for families to use for vacation, retreat, and reunion. The conference center presented here as an example of this style of gathering is the religious summer community at Montreat, North Carolina, founded in 1907 by the Presbyterian Church in the United States (the "Southern Presbyterians"). Montreat and other similar centers provide the most elaborate version of the Protestant pilgrim shrine, where the symbols of sacred place— the rural Utopian community (the nearest human equivalent to the "city of God")—are overlaid with those of the family as a sacred vessel through which the faith is carried down through the generations. The powerful messages of teaching and preaching interpret the universe in ways that are Biblically derived and doctrinally correct according to the Presbyterian vision of reality.

In both the denominational conference centers—the high shrines for Protestant pilgrimage—and in the life of the pilgrim way associated with the shrines of the medieval church, nonhierarchical forms predominate and the life-style of the journey to the sacred center plunges the participants into the state of ritual liminality. For individuals who have long ago left their rural past behind to follow the call of profession and individual goals, the conference centers, with their attendant family summer communities, become a reestablishment of the set of ties and obligations that the medieval pilgrim left behind when he or she took up the pilgrim way. In all the various forms of kin-religious gatherings I have studied, the individual Protestant is performing an act that is the opposite of his or her Roman Catholic counterpart. The Protestant pilgrim is seeking to travel *back into* sets of ritual relationships that the classical medieval pilgrim was traveling *away from*.

In the periodic communities that are created by the cyclical ceremonies of Protestant pilgrimage, the activities, symbols, rules, and beliefs of the culture are unfolded and take on life. In these contexts the children are exposed to the ritual performances, oral tradition, and informal lore that is part of the culture of the people; young adults regularly are presented with suitable marriage mates in highly charged emotional settings; the speeches and sermons, music, kinship concern, and family histories all unite to construct a powerful performance of a culture's understanding of itself.

The model of pilgrimage I am suggesting provides a useful way of understanding these Protestant kin-religious gatherings as more than simply an interesting pattern of social networks or, even more simply, as a set of old customs gradually dying away. These assemblages are so visible in the summer and so important to their participants that they cry out to the social scientist for explanation. I explain them here as part of an overall cultural system. Protestant pilgrimage in postindustrial society, I maintain, presents a set of meanings and symbols that contrast to those of medieval Christianity and later Roman Catholicism while holding a comparable position in the social process. Both hold a position of being liminoid phenomena similar to the liminality of initiation in a tribal society. They form periods of *communitas*, or liminality, alternating with periods of structure in the sum of ordered obligations and constraints that form each particular culture. Both styles of pilgrimage express alternation between rural and urban, *communitas* and structure, kin-based society and individualized society, yet each stands in its own setting as a symbolic statement of central cultural meaning. The Turners have used the term *liminoid* to describe

> the many genres found in modern industrial leisure that have features resembling those of liminality. . . . They are . . . akin to the ritually liminal, but not identical with it. . . . These genres develop most characteristically outside the central economic and political processes, along their margins, on their interfaces, in their tacit dimensions. They are plural, fragmentary, . . . experimental, idiosyncratic, quirky, subversive, utopian, and characteristically produced and consumed by identifiable individuals, in contrast to liminal phenomena which are often anonymous or divine in origin.　　　(Turner and Turner 1978:253)

Turner says that the classical pilgrimage "succeeds the major initiation rites of puberty in tribal societies as the dominant historical form. It is, indeed, the ordered antistructure of patrimonial feudal systems" (Victor Turner 1974a:182). I am suggesting that the Protestant pilgrimage to reunions, homecomings, and institutional denominational centers—all shrines within the pilgrimage complex—is indeed the ordered antistructure of the bureaucratic rational system of postindustrial Protestantism. The pilgrimage becomes for the homeward-bound Protestants the symbolic equivalent of what Geertz has seen in the Balinese shadow play and in the cockfight as "a story they tell themselves about themselves" (Geertz 1973:448), and in so doing they create their culture anew with each succeeding summer.

CHAPTER TWO

The Open-Air Service as Cultural Expression—Themes of Ecclesiastical Inversion

PILGRIMAGES, as other forms of cultural and social symbolic expression, are not created out of thin air at the sudden whim of people or groups; they are generated and continued as a part of ongoing historical and symbolic processes, and they are constructed out of an existing symbolic inventory. The reunion complex of Protestant pilgrimages has grown over time from a number of historical processes and is made up of symbols that have deep roots in the Celtic and Anglo-Saxon culture shared by the American descendants of Scots and Ulster Scots. Among these symbols are those of the regenerative power of nature and of rural worship, especially worship in the open air. A distinctive feature of all the kin-religious gatherings in the Southern United States—whether based on ancestors and kin, sacred place, or ideational community—is that the gatherings have historically taken place outdoors. The tradition of the open-air service, the pattern I call *folk liturgy*, is an important tradition among American Southerners and one that fits into older Celtic and Anglo-Saxon cultural forms.[1]

I have claimed that the reunion complex in the Southern United States, and in Protestant culture generally, makes a comment on Protestant culture in the modern world in the same way that Roman Catholic pilgrimage makes a comment on Catholic culture, especially that of the medieval world. In addition, the Protestant world view and its corresponding pilgrimage system form a commentary *on* and an inversion *of* the Catholic world view and pilgrimage system. Deeply embedded in the history of Western Europe one finds the recurrent conflict between hierarchical forms of society and nonhierarchical forms; between the corporate authoritative control of the Established Church and the loosely knit communal system of polity in the small community form of congregationalism; between the kings, princes, and feudal domains and the local and tribal domains of indigenous farmers or peasants. Many of the antiestablishment groups have called on the symbolism of the open fields and of nature as an important mobilizing motif in their campaigns in the battle against enclosed liturgical forms of worship.

The story of the interaction between the nonhierarchical Celtic and Saxon Scots and English with Roman and then Norman representation of hierarchical forms of power and religion is a story of a symbolic battle. It is also the story of the interplay between two civilizations, or cultural worlds—that of Mediterranean Europe and Rome, gradually expressed throughout the courts of France and of England and Scotland, and that of the indigenous Northern European cultural world of local tradition. The world of the Great Tradition included, in addition to the court, the cities and cathedral towns, the mercantile establishment tied to the court through royal burghs and royal companies, and the network of powerful families controlling courts, armies, and landholdings in the feudal system; of course, it also was tied together functionally and symbolically by the Roman Catholic Church. The Folk Tradition (Redfield 1941) was a world of scattered farms and hamlets, local markets, kin groups, and communities headed by local chieftains or kin group elders; its religious life included various pre-Christian elements in its syncretic versions of Roman Christianity brought by early missionaries and monks.

In understanding why the Protestant version of pilgrimage developed as it did, resulting in a reunion complex expressing themes that are Protestant and also anti-Catholic, one is assisted by viewing this complex within a larger pattern of history. I present the outdoor service here as a social type, fitting into the tradition of the folk cultures of Scotland and the North of England, points of origin for significant proportions of the population of the American South.

The Outdoor Tradition in Scottish Religion

The history of the introduction of Roman Christianity into Saxon and Celtic Britain is the story of a constant struggle of the church fathers to "civilize" the pagans, to obliterate their folk religion, and to bring into the sacred cover of the indoor church the numerous outdoor festivals and ceremonies accompanying indigenous belief systems. During the early centuries of the effort, seasonal festivals were gradually converted into saints' days, indigenous ritual forms were gradually turned into folk pastimes and secularized; others were subsumed later into medieval drama. The players and minstrels became professionalized as actors, removing them from the religious category. At the same time, however, the people's adherence to religious outdoor services of worship and to assemblies at sacred places such as stones, wells, trees, and glens continued to be important into the medieval period and beyond. These practices were continually fought by the Church through the centuries.

One strategy by the Church for dealing with the problem of pagan religious practices was to tolerate these alongside the practices of Roman Catholicism and to hope for the gradual disappearance of the earlier forms in the face of the missionary efforts. In a famous letter to Augustine, missionary in Southern England in 601 A.D., Pope Gregory stated the Church policy as that of "weaning the people gradually from their heathen practices. . . ." "The places of the pagan gods," says Gregory, "are to be purified, not destroyed, and the sacred places of the people are to be used for new worship." In his *Historia Ecclesia* the venerable Bede quotes Gregory's letter as stating that "The people may celebrate in arbors made of boughs of trees and built around the church whose especial festival is being celebrated" (Baskerville 1920:22–23).

The Church strategy changed in later centuries to one that was not so tolerant. Numerous decrees were sent out to ban the outdoor assemblies in an attempt to wipe out "pagan survivals." In commenting on this attempt, of which the ultimate goal was to substitute the church edifice for the outdoor shrines, Baskerville notes that "A large number of decrees deal with the practice of pagan rites at stones, wells, and trees." In certain documents of this period "the uttering of vows in arbors are forbidden," and "Northumbriam Priest Laws prescribe penalties for gatherings at stones, trees, and wells. . ." (Baskerville 1920:65). By the twelfth and thirteenth centuries a whole series of decrees were enacted by the Church to forbid the gathering of folk in cemeteries and sacred groves. Baskerville comments on the continuation of outdoor places of worship by the folk in the following statement.

> The decree of Gregory in 601 that the people should build their arbors and hold their feasts in the space around the churches probably established the cemetery as the "sacred place" of the folk and finally as their general meeting place. It is clear from the denunciations of the church fathers that at the beginning of the thirteenth century the cemeteries were the sites for the common halls, and the regular places for trials, ordeals, and town meetings as well as for the games of the folk.
>
> (Baskerville 1920:65)

It is hardly surprising to find that in the wake of the Scottish Reformation when the established church—albeit this time the Church of Scotland—again set out to quell antiestablishment forms of worship and assembly, the target was the outdoor assemblage. This time it was in the form of the "outdoor preaching" or "outdoor communions" that abounded during the early seventeenth century in Lowland Scotland.

In the historical accounts of Scottish church conflict, one is struck by the recurring theme of outdoor versus indoor sites for worship, preaching, and communion services. Official church histories emphasize the "field preachings" and other outdoor services in the early 1600s but, long before this time, the Celtic Church in Scotland's Southwest possessed a tradition of outdoor worship and rural retreats. Later this region was, in fact, the cradle of Reformation participation. Many of the original Reformers in the Protestant Church of Scotland were from the South and Southwest of Scotland, where the Scottish Church had a history of over 1000 years.

The Celtic Church, founded by St. Ninian in the fourth century in the Southwest, emphasized nature and the beauty of the outdoors. Withdrawal to the woods or lakes for meditation by groups of Christians was a regular part of the liturgical tradition, according to Chadwick (1963). Chadwick states that the Celtic saints were sanctified not by ecclesiastical authority but by their own daily lives and the respect of their fellow Christians. If sacred

stones, wells, and trees of pre-Christian religious forms were originally a problem to this branch of early Christian tradition, they
were gradually assimilated. Stones, wells, and trees were incorpo-
rated into a Christian form of worship that emphasized the beauty
of nature and the virtues of the simpler outdoor rural life.

Between the seventh and the twelfth centuries the Scottish
church remained isolated from English and continental authority or
contact, developing its own indigenous Celtic Christianity and
nurturing its own indigenous priesthood. Social historian Christopher Smout characterizes this time in the following description.

> The church had nominally accepted Roman in place of Celtic usages at
> the start of the eighth century, following the church in the north of
> England after the Synod of Whitby in 664. Then came the Norse
> encirclement, and contact with the outside world virtually ceased. The
> Scottish church developed characteristics of ritual and discipline that
> were out of line with those practised in England and on the Conti-
> nent.   (Smout 1969:20)

Smout refers to the style of monasticism practiced by the Celtic
Church as being of the "relatively disorganized 'desert hermit'
type, typified by the Culdean community on St. Serfs Island in
Loch Leven" (Smout 1969:24).

Celtic Christianity formed a local version of the Christianity
that was developing in Rome. Even though the Roman church
sought to establish its authority over its faraway missionary
branches, the Celtic Church remained separate and developed its
own traditions from the fourth to the seventh centuries. It was, of
course, during this period that Roman political authority was
eroded in Britain and that Rome as a power finally withdrew.
Scotland had never been under Rome's control, remaining essentially in the hands of local Celtic princes and chieftans; in England
these centuries saw the rise to power of numerous Saxon principali-
ties. In the religious realm, the Celtic Church established its own
customs, traditions, and practices, calling heavily on native Celtic
and Saxon local religious beliefs and behaviors. One of these was
the use of the outdoors as a worship setting and the reverence for
nature that is one aspect of withdrawal into monastic communities
and rural retreats for periodic renewal. In the Synod of Whitby in
664, the struggle between Roman authority and Celtic local auton-

omy was temporarily resolved with a small victory for Rome; but it was also the occasion for the assertion of Celtic tradition through the first writing down of the Celtic customs, saints' lives, and other lore by the monks so that these would not be lost (Chadwick 1963:152). The struggle between these two powers in both religious and political arenas has become deeply ingrained in the history of Western Europe—Rome became the symbol of Mediterranean civilization and classical cultural traditions in both court and church; the local and communal versions of church and authority symbolized the Northern European cultural traditions of Celtic and Saxon peoples.

Throughout the next centuries these themes of local and communal authority, natural rural beauty, and emphasis on certain sacred places became central to the Scottish outdoor worship service as a liturgical form. Three basic types of outdoor religious gatherings have been persistent (or have been repeatedly reinvented). One well-known type is that of the Covenanting Meeting of the 1600s, a second is that of the Communion Season of the 1700s and 1800s, and a third is that of the conventicle, or outdoor service, of the present day.

The Covenanters and Outdoor Services

Outdoor worship services became a vehicle for social protest during the period following the formation of the Protestant Church in Scotland in 1560. In the second half of the sixteenth century and throughout the seventeenth century, war ensued between the Reformers (later the Covenanters) and the Established Church (headed by the Crown). During this period, various ministers from time to time withdrew from their pulpits or were excommunicated by order of the King and the Church courts. Open fields and woods became the site both for pulpits and for military musters.

The term Covenanters has been used by historians to refer primarily to a religious-political group forming in opposition to the Crown and the established Church of Scotland after the signing of the National Covenant in Greyfriars Church in Edinburgh in 1638. The Covenanters represented the Scottish tradition of non-hierarchical church structure, with the governance resting in assemblies of ministers, bishops, and presbyters; the National Covenant was a statement against the formation and continuance of an episcopacy in the Church of Scotland, of which the King had declared himself supreme head. The meetings of those who followed the Covenanters and their protest movement were necessarily held in secret, often in glades, dells, and forest glens. In taking to the open air and holding their services in the woods, the Covenanters were calling on the powerful symbolism of nature and the natural world, the earlier worship places of the sacred groves of Celtic peoples, and on the images of Celtic monasticism creating a concept of saintliness associated with the piety of ordinary individuals.

In his history of Scotland, T. C. Smout points out that the original signers of the National Covenant included aristocrats and nobles, but that eventually these politically and economically powerful figures became aligned with the government and with the established Church of Scotland that was created following the end of the Covenanting Wars. Smout notes, however, that there was continued "widespread support for the Covenanting movement after 1660 among the humble. . ." (Smout 1969:64), especially in the Lowlands, "at least if we can judge by the reverence in which the names and works of dissenting Covenanters were held in districts such as the Lothians in the eighteenth century." Smout goes on to say of these ongoing activities in the Lowlands that in certain areas, including Ayrshire, Dumfriesshire, and Galloway, and in the central Borders "the excluded ministers were able to gather a following together significant enough to enable a secret church to be kept going." We find that it is in these regions, especially in Dumfriesshire and Galloway, that the Covenanters "met out of doors at field preachings where hundreds came together to hear their heroes" (Smout 1969:64).

Local histories disagree on where and when the earliest of the Covenant meetings, later known as Conventicles, took place. All agree that the movement began or came to the surface in Southwest Scotland. The Covenant preachers were ousted from the church officially in 1661, and official curates were inducted to take their places (Brown 1960). At the same time field preaching became a capital offense. Ministers were required by law to live more than 20 miles away from the parishes they had formerly served. There were many bloody battles, and thousands died.

In writing of the Galloway region, a local historian describes the situation as follows.

> In 1662 Gabriel Semple, minister of Kirkpatrick-Durham was driven from his church . . . he conducted services in Corsock House until his audiences became too large, then in the garden, and finally in the open fields. . . . (Robertson 1963:153)

Robertson gives the figure for excommunicated ministers as 350 throughout Scotland during this period. The so-called "Black Act" of 1670 made even the attendance at Conventicles punishable by death and, at the same time, leveled heavy fines on those who did not attend the parish church where they were registered.

In spite of these legal sanctions, attendance swelled, with the most famous service of the period coming in 1678 at Irongray Churchyard, drawing several thousand to take communion in the open air. Robertson describes the setting at this famous service in this way.

> The tables were four parallel rows of long flat oblong stones, each row about 20 yards in length. At one end there was a circular cairn of stones several feet high where the officiating minister stood. The Communion was served in relays to several hundred communicants at a time, and the service continued all through the day and into the evening.
> (Robertson 1963:170)

Barr states that the services at Irongray lasted three days, "a great 'open-air communion service . . . the rude stones forming the communion tables and the seats" (Barr 1947:175). These covenanting communions set the pattern for a tradition that was to last for several centuries.

The Outdoor Communion

In the eighteenth century, the century of early manufacturing and of migration to the colonies, the open-air tradition continued as a form of joint meeting among the scattered residents of a country parish. "Communion Season" is referred to throughout the literature of the eighteenth century as that time in the summer, in May, or in October when the country parish held its own particular gathering. Each parish had a set time for the holding of its Communion, and the members of adjoining parishes were eligible to attend if they wished.

Since the days of the Reformation, one method of bounding off the group who received the Communion together was the issuance of tokens, small circles of carved wood carrying the seal of a particular parish. These would be issued by the minister to communicants in the parish; when the person moved, he or she would take the token to present to the minister in the new parish as evidence of good character and church membership. A verbal and spatial statement known as "fencing the tables" consisted of the reading of the Scriptures that deny the sacraments to those who are not true believers and at the same time actually separating the tables from direct access of the people by elders stationed to receive people's tokens as proof of their status in the community of the redeemed.

From a museum exhibit in Kirkudbright the following information gives a picture of how serious the exclusion process was.

> In a parish in Perthshire in 1791, 2361 people took communion at one service . . . . It was customary in those days for the communion table to be enclosed within a wooden pailing to keep out non-communicants. . . . An elder stood at one end to collect tokens.
> (Edmiston 1974:1)

A local historian examined the kirk records for the Parish Kirk of Hawick for the period 1711–1725 and found numerous references to the Communion Season. According to Vernon (1900), prior to 1700 the Kirk Session was strict in seeing that tokens were given only to members of their own parish. Subsequently, however, it became a common custom for people of adjacent parishes to come in large numbers to any church in the district where the Communion was to be observed. In order to provide the visitors with tokens, the minister of the parish would supply the ministers of adjoining parishes with tokens several weeks before. It was the custom of the country folk to attend several Communions, and farm servants contracted with their employers that they be allowed to attend a specified number of fairs and Communions per year. It was a social occasion where one visited with friends and kinfolk and partook of the preaching and the bread and wine of the sacrament itself.

The service was held in the kirkyard. Vernon found references in the church records to payments made to tradesmen for putting up tents and tables. He notes the picturesque scene created by the "tables laid out on trestles on the grass." At Hawick the Communion Season was the first Sunday after the gathering of the harvest, in October. The gathering lasted three days; Saturday was the Fast Day, the Communion was held on the Sabbath, and a service of thanksgiving was held on Monday. Because the Communion Season in Hawick was in October, the weather was too cool for sleeping in the open fields; travelers either came early in the morning and went home late at night, or they stayed over in local inns. The visiting ministers slept at the manse (Vernon 1900:44).

Another local historian describes the Communion Season at Yarrow in the early 1800s in the following words.

> Our own Communion was one of our happiest seasons. There were holidays and no lessons. There were friends about the house, and good dinners . . . . . . My Father had just *one* Communion in the year, in the beginning of August (latterly on the second Sabbath of July). In this he conformed to the custom of those days; and, I believe, was influenced by the feeling prevalent in many quarters still, that it had the sanction of the Mosaic dispensation in its yearly Passover, and the belief that it was observed with more solemnity than it would have been had it been celebrated more frequently. (Russell 1886:172)

Russell states that the services before and after the Communion were a major focus of emphasis and, in fact, the gathering was commonly known as "The Preaching" among the country folk. The sequence of events is described by Russell for the Communion of his own childhood, held by his father as minister.

> The Sabbath service was a protracted one. It began at 10:30 and with one hour and a quarter of interval, did not close till about 7:00 P.M.; so that those who came from the extremeties of the parish, . . . had to start at an early and return at a late hour. There were seven full communion tables. Refreshments of bread and cheese and milk were provided in the kitchen for all comers of the people generally; a bowl put in the "ministers' well" for those who liked a cooling beverage of spring water; bread and ale in the barn, furnished by some of the publicans of the parish; . . . and refreshments in the dining room and parlour of the manse for the farmers and their families. The ministers and elders dined at the manse during the interval. A sumptuous "Monday's dinner" to which some of the principal parishioners were invited, completed the service of carnal things. (Russell 1886:177)

During the gathering, there were many who, according to contemporary reports, became quite rowdy with the mixture of fellowship and strong drink. Russell refers to the situation in a certain parish—not his native Yarrow—where in 1785 he considers the assembly to have "degenerated" into a social occasion.

> . . . the crowds needed refreshments, "lest they should faint by the way" . . . baps of bread and ale were planted round the churchyard dyke (wall). All day long there was an oscillation between the one and the other.
>
> When a popular preacher mounted the rostrum, the people all flocked to the tent; when a *wauf* hand turned up, the tide was all the other way. . . . The tent was deserted, and the baps and barrels carried the day. There was an unceasing contest between the spiritual and the spirituous—the holy day was turned into a holiday. . . .
>
> (Russell 1886:8)

It is the social occasion and merriment of the outdoor gatherings that led the poet Robert Burns to compare the event to a country fair (Burns 1795). There are many similarities if one examines carefully the social meaning and the sequence of events. It cannot be ignored that the two appear side by side in the farm labor contracts of the period in terms of guaranteed time off for leisure pastimes. On the other hand, the Communion cannot be passed over as merely a social gathering for visiting with neighbors. Over the centuries it took on a symbolic meaning, ceremonially connecting the living community with its past in the Covenant tradition and in the feasts of the Old Testament. The beauties of the countryside were extolled as being a part of God's creation, and the sacredness of the place itself was emphasized by references to previous holy men holding the pulpit of the church and to the Godly lives of the ancestors who were buried in the graveyard.

The symbolic significance of the open-air Communions is touched on in this poem written in the nineteenth century by a Hawick parishioner. It underlines the importance of the past and of the continuing community of people within one parish throughout the ongoing generations.

> Slow the people round the table
> Outspread, white as mountain sleet,
> Gather, the blue heavens above them,

> And their dead beneath their feet;
> There in perfect reconcelement
> Death and life immortal meet.
> Noiseless round that fair white table
> 'Mid their fathers thombstones spread
> Hoary-headed elders moving,
> Bear the hallowed wine and bread,
> While devoutly still the people
> Low in prayer bow the head.
> (by "Principal Shairp" of Hawick,
> quoted in Vernon 1900:45)

As late as 1845 we know that open-air Communion services were routinely celebrated annually, at least in the Southwest. In the *Second Statistical Account of Scotland*, published in 1845, the Reverend Cullen and the Reverend Murray describe the Balmaclellan church building as "much too small for sacramental occasions, when worship is performed in the open air. . ." (McElroy 1971).

After the turn of the century in both the Southwest and in the Borders, however, there seemed to be a shift in the Communion into the inside of the church building. Informants throughout the region were unable to recall seeing an outdoor Communion service in their lifetimes.[2] This may be partly due to the gradual increase of influence of the Church of Scotland General Assembly in reuniting smaller segmented factions into an overall national church structure. The official policy is now to hold Communion four times a year, or even once a month, and to hold it within the prescribed indoor liturgical form of the Church of Scotland.

Jubilees, Anniversaries, and Conventicles

Outdoor services after 1850, through the present day, take on the form of anniversaries or jubilees celebrating the anniversary of a covenanting battle, the anniversary of the founding of the church, or the anniversary of the coming of the present minister. The two latter types are often celebrated on 25- and 50-year anniversaries, thus adopting the name "jubilee." The outdoor commemorations of covenanting battles are held annually on the date of the battle and are known as Conventicles or, by the people, simply as "out-door services." Again, a recurring theme is the tie to the past and to the continuous community of God's people who have inhabited this particular place over the unfolding years.

Frequently a local history is written by the pastor to com-memorate these anniversaries—especially those on centenaries. One such local history written in 1889 describes a jubilee held to com-memorate the anniversary of a minister's ordination—apparently the seventy-fifth, although it is unclear whether the honoree was alive or dead at his celebration.

> An outdoor meeting under a tent held to commemorate the third jubilee of the ordination of Rev. John Hunter . . . at Gateshaw Brae . . . a crowd of 2000 from all Border Presbyteries, from the Free Church, from the Presbyterian Church of England.
>
> Some were present who had attended a similar gathering fifty years ago.   (Tait 1889:18)

Apparently Gateshaw Brae was chosen because of its long history of having been the scene of outdoor services (a *brae* in old Scots is a small hill or a hillside). It is especially mentioned in the outdoor meetings held during the Secession of 1737. In this partic-ular Secession, those who wanted to retain the right to choose ministers (i.e., to leave this in the hands of the congregation and of "heads of families") rebelled against the General Assembly. The official body had ruled that this right was to be restricted "to heritors, elders, magistrates and town councillors in burghs and to heritors and elders in country parishes" (Tait 1889:34). Again, we see the communal, antihierarchical forces taking to the open air.

Throughout the splitting and realigning of factions that marks the history of the Church of Scotland, the rebellious groups repeat-edly invoked open-air symbolism. A number of outdoor services in summertime today commemorate activities of Covenanters and their organizational (or antiorganizational) counterparts. In the Lammermuir hills there are several meeting spots made famous by protestors who withdrew from the Parish Kirk at Lauder in 1747 to form an outdoor group affiliated with the movement known as the "AntiBurghers." Tait (1889) refers to them as "the lineal representatives of the Covenanters." Another famous outdoor ser-vice is held annually at St. Mary's Loch at an old graveyard. The gathering is known as a "blanket preaching." The rhetoric of the preaching at summer gatherings of these types often includes references to the previous generations who "fought oppression." Among the ministers inside the established town churches and in the theological schools at Edinburgh and Glasgow, the meetings are largely scoffed at or ignored. If noticed at all, it is with the cryptic comment of one established churchman who referred to the blanket preaching as "an old tradition being dragged along."

Outdoor and Indoor—Some Recurring Themes

In this sketchy reconstruction of over 300 years of outdoor services, it is possible to discern several repetitive themes and a number of structural regularities. Consistently, outdoor services are associated with the rebellion against authority and hierarchy represented by the established church. They represent a political statement as well as a theological statement. The emphasis is on nature and sacred places, many of which are also connected with the sanctification of hallowed ground by battles for "freedom" or "against oppression." Heroes and ancestors are honored in the preaching, in the celebration of anniversaries, and in the holding of gatherings at the gravestones of well-known Covenanting figures. The collective community of the ancestors are honored in the act of holding services in the graveyard "with the dead around their feet." The participating group is distinct and bounded—in the past by fenced tables, in the present by selective knowledge and an interest in finding out the repetitive exact day of the gathering and attending it.

Contrasting to the antiestablishment expressions of the outdoor services are the staid, stalwart formal services held inside the established Church of Scotland. The pattern of liturgy remains essentially unchanged over the centuries, and the doctrine preached is the approved version of the intellectually refined Calvinism that is taught in the seminaries at Glasgow and Edinburgh. There are no bishops and no patronage in the modern Church of Scotland. Each congregation chooses its own minister and sends representatives to the regional presbytery and to the general assembly. The congregations are, however, subject to regulation through church law as handed down by the general assembly. Whereas the minister is "called" by the congregation, he is not a member of it but of the presbytery and subject to his ultimate regulation by the presbytery and general assembly. The system of government, theological orthodoxy, and organizational structure of the Church of Scotland is both indoors and closed.

In his study of social movements, which he calls "primitive" or "archaic" in Europe and in nineteenth century Britain, Eric Hobsbawm (1959) identifies a number of political undertones in the rise of Protestant sectarianism in the towns and cities of England during the height of industrialism between 1800 and 1851. It was these newly urbanized, formerly peasant farmers and the descendants of earlier urbanized peasants who embraced emotional, affective, and antihierarchical forms of religion in Britain, while their cousins in the American former colonies were embracing revivalistic religion on the American frontier. Hobsbawm classifies the movements to which he gives attention as expressions of social protest and of social agitation aimed at the elite and empowered classes of society by the disenfranchised. His types include social banditry as in Robin Hood-style movements, peasant millenarianism, rural secret societies, and urban sectarianism. The outdoor gatherings I have described for early Scotland fit into this classification and are a form of culturally framed social protest as well as a religious assembly. The fact that this particular form was seized on by the American revivalists on the western frontier of upstate New York in the early 1800s and in the fields of Kentucky and Tennessee is not accidental. It provides a clear example of the persistence of cultural forms and their reinvention for social and political purposes.

Outdoor Services in the Early United States

The dissenting tradition associated with the Covenanters of the Lowlands of Scotland found its way to the American colonies in the migration of both Scots and Ulster Scots. Scottish settlers from the Lowlands were planted in the North of Ireland in the early 1600s by the English King. Those who emigrated to the American colonies became known in America as Scotch-Irish. They formed a significant proportion of the population of the middle colonies and of the back country of the Valley of Virginia and the Carolina Piedmont. According to E. T. Thompson, "There were Scotch-Irish settlements in Maryland as early as 1680; in South Carolina as early as 1682." By the time of the American Revolution, he says, "there were approximately 500,000 Scotch-Irish in America, one-sixth of the total population of the country" (Thompson 1963:42).[3]

Forces contributing to the exodus of the Scots and Ulster Scots were the combined forces of economy and of religious dissent. On the one hand, Ireland and Southern Scotland were experiencing a depression. Meanwhile, many of the long-term leases of these Scottish descendants in Ireland were falling due. If the large landowners were willing to renew leases at all, it was at considerably higher rates. On the other hand, the established church was tightening its insistence on conformity. It is not surprising that the open lands of Pennsylvania, New York and, later, the Carolinas, Kentucky, and Tennessee lured hundreds of thousands of migrants to join the parade into the western frontier of America. It was this population of Lowland Scots and Ulster Scots—who have been called the "descendants of the Covenanters" by more than one religious historian—among whom the great revivals and open-field preachings became the dominant motif for worship and belief in the nineteenth century.[4] It was among the Scotch-Irish of backwoods America that the outdoor tradition flourished and became a part of the folklore of the western frontier.

Outdoor services in America took the form of field preaching, of camp meeting, and of "open-air preaching." Within the more settled congregations the people also took to the outdoors for annual outdoor communion, for "protracted meetings" and for gatherings in the summertime known as "dinner on the grounds." The worship form for these events resembles in its location, process, and political statement the form for dissent and protest against established church authority that was exemplified in the Scottish meetings of an earlier time. Like their Scottish counterparts of earlier centuries, many of the preachers for the open-air services were members of the clergy in a mainstream Protestant denomination. Their disagreement with the established church often led them to form new congregations.

Factions split away from every denomination, while the Methodist and Baptist denominations grew dramatically. The lack of rigidity in doctrinal matters and their tolerance for preachers who were not college educated placed these two denominations in line with earlier dissenting, nonhierarchical, antiestablishment movements that had also used the fields for their assembly grounds.

In the following chapters the contemporary versions of the outdoor tradition will be described. Family reunions, church homecomings, cemetery reunions, camp meetings, and denominational rural retreats today provide instances of the fact that the outdoor tradition is alive and well in America. In these events one finds all the elements of the Scottish outdoor services and of the outdoor tradition of the American frontier, but added to these themes are the themes of reunion with kinfolk and honor of the ancestors who are founders of the family or church. I have classified these gatherings together with those of the Protestant past in a common outdoor tradition and contrasted it with the indoor one of the established and hierarchical church. In doing so I do not make the claim that I have traced a full historical process through which the Scottish outdoor traditions became those of the Southern United States. Instead, I outline parallel social and cultural processes in which a distinctive type of ritual form has emerged, and I point to ways in which this ritual form is expressed in modern Protestant society.

Outdoor and Indoor Traditions:
the Open and the Closed

Within the structure and process of the outdoor services of Scotland and of frontier America there is a consistency of pattern and form that constitutes a specific liturgical tradition that is open and nonhierarchical, a tradition seen also in the Celtic Christianity of North Britain. This tradition is quite distinct from the Roman Catholic Christian version of worship, which is a closed corporate form that is hierarchical in belief and organization. While I have not claimed that the outdoor tradition is in fact Celtic or that the Southern United States has been shaped predominantly by Celtic cultural patterns, it is true that the outdoor worship as a form has persisted through many centuries in regions where Celtic Christianity was once strong and has emerged as an important figure in the overall configuration of the Protestant culture of the Southern United States. The important point is that in both North British and in Southern United States cultures there exists a folk tradition of worship and religious expression that I call *folk liturgy* that is both open and outdoors; this contrasts dramatically with the liturgy of the Great Tradition, which is indoors and closed.

Covenanting services, Communion on the churchgrounds, twentieth-century Conventicles, frontier revivals, and family, church, and cemetery reunions all can be seen as aspects of this ongoing outdoor tradition. These services and field preachings are not isolated occurrences with only particularistic, historical significance. They constitute a form of cultural expression that corresponds to certain folk cultures of Northern Britain. As such they exemplify a ritual form that finds its distinctiveness in the Christianity of Northern European Protestant tradition, in opposition to the hierarchical forms of the Established Church or the Great Tradition of Roman, Mediterranean Christianity. The social organization of the folk—that of scattered, open-country community centered in the crossroads meeting—finds itself in counterpoint with the social organization of highly stratified feudal society and of the exclusive and monopolistic structures of the burgh or town. The liturgical form of the outdoor service is the form that the populus seized on through time to express its own cultural identity in opposition to the hierarchies of both the feudal domains and the feudal-economic captivity of the towns whose form of worship was that of the traditional, indoor, hierarchical, state church.

The architectural expression of the traditional state church is the cathedral or the established parish church building with its attendant spires, bells, stained glass, arches, and pulpit raised above the congregation. Architecturally, the outdoor tradition is expressed historically in brush arbors and, in the present day, in open-sided wooden structures also called "arbors" in which the camp meeting services and memorial services in cemeteries are held. Hymns and prayers dwell not on the vertical access to God provided by priests and other intercessors but on horizontal equality of people in direct contact with their ministers, with each other, and with God—a concept known theologically as the "priesthood of believers." The communion of this outdoor tradition is made of simple food cooked by the women. It is served from a row of stationary stone or concrete tables constituting a distinctive fixed feature of Southern Protestant rural churchgrounds and many cemeteries in the country. In contrast, the Eucharist, or the communion meal of the indoor and hierarchical church is made of special consecrated elements of food prepared and served by ordained priests. The outdoor tradition celebrates family and local ancestors; stories and legends recount tales of their bravery and courage in ordinary situations. In contrast, the traditional stories and legends of the indoor church include those of Biblical figures, saints, and miracles. In the indoor church, approved doctrine and theology are the guides for correct behavior and belief; ecclesiastical history is emphasized, and the church as an institution is held up as a final authority. In contrast, the outdoor gatherings focus on individual interpretations, fellowship, communal life, and the history and tradition associated with a particular family or with a sacred place and its local heroes and meanings.

These two types of ritual forms and their contrasting structural and processural features might be seen more clearly when presented in sets of contrasting pairs of features (see Table 1).

Table 1.   Features of Indoor and Outdoor Liturgical Traditions

Indoor Tradition	Outdoor Tradition
Cathedral, church building	Open air, fields, tent, churchyard
Sanctuary	"Brush arbor," open-sided frame arbor
High altar	Stone tables in the churchyard
Priests (hierarchy of office)	Priesthood of believers (nonhierarchical)
Eucharist, consecrated food	Simple ordinary food in shared meal
Communion served by ordained priests (traditionally men)	Food served by ordinary people (often women)
Stories of saints and miracles	Stories of family, ancestors, and founders
Correct doctrine, creeds, theology	Personal faith, communal life, "fellowship"
Ecclesiastical tradition and history	Local history, family and place histories
Institutional church, ecumenical church, church as sacred	Congregation, local traditions, local sacred place

This set of contrasts reveals the presence of two distinct ideal types of ritual tradition and symbolic social expression. In presenting these contrasts in historical context, I do not imply that I am doing a history of Protestant or Catholic worship forms or that I am attempting to trace explicit historical origins of any form—these tasks I leave to the historians. I claim only that I am doing cultural anthropology—carrying out an ethnological analysis of these forms. I suggest logically opposed ideal types, types opposed structurally and processually to one another, types representing two contrastive historical and cultural traditions. These can be seen over time and space within broad European contexts and in the context of American Protestant culture. The outdoor tradition finds its most visible expression, I maintain, in the complex of gatherings I have studied in the Southern United States. In these rituals of reunion one finds not only the structural and processual opposite of Roman Catholic pilgrimage and liturgy but also an important symbolic social form for expressing and creating meanings associated with the liturgy and life of Protestantism. And the Protestant configuration of meanings is, in fact, an inversion of the Roman Catholic one.

In the folk liturgy of Protestant outdoor services we find a form for the inversion of a world—the world associated with the medieval church, with the Established State Church, the Roman Catholic Church, with hierarchical structures of religious authority and power. We also find a form for combining and expressing certain central themes of Protestantism and for commenting ritually on the contradictions and difficulties within the world of modern Protestants. The pilgrimage to gatherings based on kinship and communal life is itself a liminal phase of the modern bureaucratic and secular urban society. In other words, the complex of Protestant reunions constitutes a liminoid phenomenon, a commentary on and a nonstructured aspect of the Protestant world, a vehicle for framing Protestant meanings and resolving temporarily certain contradictions inherent to that world. It is also a process through which the symbolic universe of Protestantism is asserted and confirmed over against that of Roman Catholicism and of the traditional church. Protestant pilgrimage is liminal to the Protestant world. Catholic pilgrimage is liminal to the Catholic world. And the first world is an inversion of the second.

The validation for these assertions lies in the ethnographic data. The kin-religious gatherings of the American South speak for themselves to provide evidence for the existence of the structural and symbolic relationships I have claimed. Their language is one that can be heard and understood as they unfold ethnographically in the pages that follow.

PART TWO

Pilgrimages

CHAPTER THREE

Family Enshrined—
The Family Reunion

EVERY SUMMER thousands of Southerners attend gatherings of relatives known as family reunions. The reunion as a type of event is, in fact, known throughout the United States and in many areas of the world where the Scots and their descendants have migrated. The reunion is styled out of a symbolic inventory shared by other outdoor services of worship and of kinship affirmation, and to those who attend the reunion of all the descendants of a common ancestor it takes on the aura of a sacred event, hallowing the kin group and the living family through an intricate symbolic expression of Protestant culture.

The Family Reunion

Every year since the early 1930s on the third Sunday in July, the Worthy family has gathered under the trees at the old camp meeting ground in North Georgia known as Clear Creek. By Saturday morning relatives have already begun to arrive and to unpack to stay overnight with one of the families who live nearby or to stay over at the family "tent," a rough cabin that stands with other family tents in a circle around the aging, open-sided arbor, the central building of the campgrounds. Even earlier, members of the two or three large families who have remained in the area have been working at the tent and at the campgrounds, airing out beds and blankets, putting new sawdust on the floor of the tent, making ready the barbecue grills for Saturday's preliminary cookout, and mowing the grass around the open-air tables and in the clearing where the men and youngsters will play softball on Sunday afternoon. Men from the local families will cook the hamburgers on Saturday for those who come early; local women will make a dozen freezers of homemade ice cream in favorite flavors; new arrivals will bring cakes, cookies, and cupcakes. On the Saturday before the reunion Sunday there is great relaxation and enjoyment in greeting one another and sharing news and gossip from the year. All the preparation has been done, and the reunion is ready to begin.

The traditional narrative that is given as the reason for the reunion tells the story of "all the children and grandchildren of John Worthy." An older woman in the family will be called on to explain the background for the benefit of the children and the visitor. She traditionally begins:

> Old John Worthy and his wife, Mary, came to North Georgia from Carolina in the 1840's and started a farm. They had eight children. Five lived to adulthood—John, Jr. who took over the farm as a young man to support his mother and the younger children after his father died; David, who became a lawyer and moved into the town nearby; young Mary, who married James Hall, who inherited a neighboring farm; Virginia, who married a Methodist minister and moved about with him in various pastorates; and little George, who went to seek his fortune in the West—in Texas, I think.   (traditional narrative)

The story will be told again and again over the years to the children, to the newcomers by marriage, and to all those who read the family history that was published some years ago by a local press and sold to the family members. The story is retold each year in symbolic form through the gathering itself, to reestablish familial ties among the descendants of these original pioneers. The original siblings have, of course, long since died and gone to join the saints in the church graveyard three miles down the road; but their children are the ones who played together on the creek during the camp meeting and who grew up as cousins. It is these now elderly people who have founded and perpetuated the reunion.

On Sunday morning the campground begins to take on life as soon as the sun is up. Those who have slept in the rude beds of the tent loft are relieved to be out on the benches on the porch, sipping coffee under the tin roof. Bacon is sizzling in the kitchen, and the toddlers are being fed breakfast by their mothers. Gradually, the pace quickens as cars begin to arrive and unload their goods down by the tables under the trees, where the noon meal will take place. Large, galvanized washtubs of ice and soft drinks are strategically placed, great metal water coolers appear on the table ends, and someone nails a bottle opener to a tree, where it has been nailed for reunion every year in the memory of this generation. One woman spreads out plastic table covers, and another puts out the covered cakes and cookies remaining from the night before. As more and more people arrive, the table fills with dishes and plates, pans and casseroles holding fried chicken, potato salad, ham, cheese grits, squash casserole, baked beans, homemade rolls, triangular pimento cheese sandwiches made from store-bought bread with the crust cut off, more cakes—chocolate, coconut, and angelfood—and pies— pecan, lemon meringue, and chess. When the dishes are uncovered later, the food will create a vivid collage of yellows and browns, dotted with the bright, bright red of fresh, sliced tomatoes and the new green of garden lettuce. For a time, the covers remain tightly closed as each new relative who appears is hugged and kissed and assisted with the lifting out of mixed cargoes of food and folding chairs, blankets and playpens.

As noon approaches, the arrivals have slowed and the activity of readying the table has quickened. A signal from one of the older men of a local family brings on complete quiet for a prayer blessing the food and the family. The minister in the family, who has said the blessing, pronounces the "Amen," and the clusters of chatting people merge imperceptibly into two slow lines, moving bit by bit down the sides of the tables, past the opened containers, filling their plates with the dishes they know well from childhood, the foods they have eaten at reunions for many years. The specialities of each mother, grandmother, and aunt are present today, each person bringing only her most famous and successful dishes. Folding chairs and blankets are pulled into circles with the hard wooden benches that line up in the shade; couples with their young children eat happily with parents and grandparents. The spouse who "married in" is quiet because he or she remains only a newcomer, not "blood kin," and will always be marginal in this transgenerational group bounded by family ties and held together by common experience and common stories.

The meal goes on for a long while, lazily extending into second desserts and another glass of iced tea. A smallish older woman moves from cluster to cluster with a book of photos, several men get up and regroup at the fringe to talk about the price of cotton and the upcoming election, children begin to play chase, and a youth brings out a bat and softball. By now the table is covered again, this time completely by clean white cloths draped over all the food to keep away the flies. The young mothers who are cousins share talk of their children, while their own mothers, who are sisters and sisters-in-law, sit nearby and discuss their own lives and the lives of each other's children. In the bed of a nearby pickup truck, backed into the circle earlier, a tiny girl sleeps contentedly on an old patchwork quilt, lulled by the hum of quiet conversation punctuated by laughter.

By late afternoon the families within the family are saying their goodbyes. The cars and trucks have begun to disappear one by one. In the quiet July heat the remaining few women clear away their casseroles and take up the plastic cloths from the long concrete tables. The washtubs will go back to town tonight, and the bottle opener will be removed from the tree until next year.

At the Walker family reunion, not too many miles away at the old Walker family homeplace, the same activities will have gone on the first Sunday in July. Along the tables outside the Clear Creek Methodist Church the Kings will gather next Sunday. On every Sunday during the summer at the campground a different family will go through the same traditional ceremony; a different cabin will be opened each Saturday and closed again on Sunday night. The Davises will have had a family meeting during the Saturday part of the gathering to discuss business matters and to elect officers, and on Sunday there will have been a special service up on the hillside in the old family burial ground. There, the master of ceremonies every year calls on each family head to introduce the children and grandchildren and their spouses and to note specially any new babies born during the year; prayers are said and speeches made about the family and its traditions. At the King reunion there will be pictures of the honored ancestors adorning the church altar during the Sunday service, and names of the Kings who were prominent church founders will be printed in the bulletin. After the service, family members visit the graveyard. Throughout the South in summer other families will gather for reunions at other places, carrying out the same kinds of activities, honoring their ancestors and their membership in the greater family in similar ways.

The reunion of the Williams family was described for an anthropology student by a woman who had participated throughout her life. She described her family reunion in the following words.

My Grandfather died in 1927. Grandma, Uncle Robert and Aunt Ema lived in the homeplace. In 1936 they invited the direct descendants of John G. Williams to come to the homeplace for a reunion. The John G. Williams reunion was begun that day, and continues to be held each year the first Sunday in July. The name of the reunion was later shortened to the Williams Reunion, but by then everybody knew if you were not a direct descendant of John G. Williams you were not invited regardless of what your name might be. After a few years the reunion was moved to Joe Eldon Williams' house, son of John G. Williams. Uncle Eldon's house is about a mile up the road from the homeplace. The reunion has continued to be held there every year since, . . .

Uncle Eldon's son, Ronald, who lives just up the road from Uncle Eldon's homeplace, has continued to make all the necessary arrangements for the approximately 140 happy, loving people who will be at the Williams Reunion unless they have a mighty good reason for not being there.

But only if you are a direct descendant. . . .   (Black 1975:3)

Being a direct descendant is defined as being one of the children, grandchildren, or great-grandchildren of one ancestor, in this case John G. Williams. The writer of this descriptive essay gives this definition.

My Grandfather John Griffin Williams and his wife Nell Davis had twelve (12) children, one of whom was my Mother, Alice Jefferson Williams, the eleventh child. John Williams and his second wife Emma Anne Phillips had four children. It is important I name them because these children and their descendants, only these children and descendants, are the people I will be writing about. . . .   (Black 1975:1)

In contrast to the reunions in which reminders are sent out and in which there is a business meeting, the reunion described for the Williams family in rural Georgia is reconvened on the same day each year without any formal correspondence; and the day's events unfold regularly without any scripting. The description goes on:

> There is no organization to the Williams Reunion. Cards sent out to remind the people to come are not necessary. It's fixed in your mind when it will be and you want to be there. You know you belong, and you know those who are there love you. There are no officers—Jim Alex does pass the hat for people to contribute whatever they want to help pay Uncle Eugene for the hogs he barbecued for the occasion. There is no speechmaking—people are too busy visiting with each other face to face. There are no name tags, because you are supposed to know everybody. (It's my responsibility to brief my children before we go.) Nobody is told what kinds of foods to bring—one knows there will be a bountiful supply and the Williams Reunion is known for its good food. One does look for Aunt Ella's carmel cake, Mary Anne's creamed style corn, Aunt Janie's sausage and biscuit. (After Aunt Janie died, Louisa, her daughter continued to bring them a few years.) There are no organized games for the children—they just all look forward to the time they will be big enough to play baseball in the back yard.
>
> (Black 1975:4)

Every reunion will include certain features that are obligatory, without which it would not be a reunion. In analyzing the Passover Seder, Meyerhoff calls these obligatory features "fixed elements" (Meyerhoff 1983). In the reunion these include the gathering of descendants of a common ancestor; the shared meal, preferably on outdoor tables adjoining a family home, a church, or a campground but possibly in a state park or community center, with the food preferably contributed by the women of each individual family; the kin visiting, greeting, and storytelling; and the recurrent time and traditional place. Other features may appear and disappear—the business meeting, the ceremony of introductions, the previous night's cookout, the visit to the graveyard, pictures, history books, and newspapers referring to ancestors or kinfolks. Other locations and other food have emerged among elite Southerners whose reunions have moved into posh locales, resorts, or country retreats or who hold their reunions at the large home of a prestigious relative; but certain basic elements of ritual form have persisted in the reunion as an event type. The reunion, in all its separate external manifestations, is an assemblage of descendants who have come together to acknowledge their ancestry and their relationship to one another as a cultural entity they call "the family."

The Family, the Kin Group, and the Ancestors

In Calvinistic Protestant culture *the family* can mean a number of things. The most common image of family is that of the individual unit of mother, father, and a few children residing together, the residential group sociologists would call a nuclear family. It can also mean the family of one of the parents with all their siblings, a family construct that would be a nuclear family of one generation in the past. A third image of the family is that of the "greater family," a unit tracing its descent backward in history to the sibling group that forms the children of one common ancestor—"old John Worthy," for instance, who came to this country or to this state in some certain year from some certain place in a previous state or country. At one level, the analysis of this greater family is a task for social anthropology, a task of discerning the kinship system that prevails here and how the various relationships are enacted in social behavior. From this viewpoint we are dealing with what I have elsewhere labeled a *cognatic descent group* (Neville 1974). A cognatic descent group could be defined as a descent group consisting of all the descendants of one common ancestor, figured through both male and female descendants. The reunion family defines itself in exactly these terms when sending out letters, writing newspaper notices, or describing its kin connections to the visiting ethnographer. And the foundation narrative is couched in these exact terms. Fox (1967) describes cognatic descent as follows.

> It is clear that in this system the numbers of my descent group will be related to me through both male *and* female links. We usually call such a system *cognatic*, "cognates" in Roman law being kin through any sex link (as opposed to agnates, for example, who are kin through male links only). (Fox 1967:47)

Cognatic descent principles, then, govern the structure and social organization of the kinship system.

The principle of a cognatic descent, an abstract notion, is seen visibly expressed in the assembly of relatives gathered for the family reunion. Those who are members of the family are those descended by "blood," that is, through natural procreation, from the ancestor. Here descent is traced through males and females equally (See Figure 1). Spouses are included as in-laws or those who have "married in" during their lifetimes. After their death they may become ancestors because of their role as progenitors of a family. While the *common ancestor* of the family is always spoken of as male, in the traditional foundation narrative he is quickly given a bride and the children's lives then are outlined. In family trees— genealogical charts—constructed to provide visual assistance for those learning about the ancestry, the wife of the founder is always included as having equal position to him. If she came from a very prominent family tree herself, her family tree is often included as separate information. The cognatic descent group is the group that assembles for a family reunion, or would ideally assemble if all the members were to be present. It includes all the separate nuclear segment families, who live scattered in various cities and towns but who gather annually. Each nuclear family is headed by a cousin whose grandparent is one of the brothers or sisters who are founders of the reunion. If the reunion has been going on for several generations, it may have been founded by the great-grandparents of the youngest named cousins, in honor of the great-great-grand-father. It is, in other words, a large extended family of persons who trace their descent back to one founding ancestor.

The cognatic descent group as assembled in the reunion family is different in structure and contrasts sharply to the nuclear family and bilateral kindred usually described as the dominant form in mainstream American life.[1] The nuclear household, consisting of father, mother, and children, keeps in touch with networks of relatives of both parents through letters and phone conversations. It gathers with various clusters of kinfolks from time to time for weddings, funerals, baptisms, and birthdays. Yet, these assemblies are based on ties of relationship outward from one person and that person's parents, the person's spouse, and the spouse's parents. The gatherings are not based on descent but on relationship to the person being honored. In other words, a bilateral kindred is "ego focused," or focused on the individual and his or her living rela-

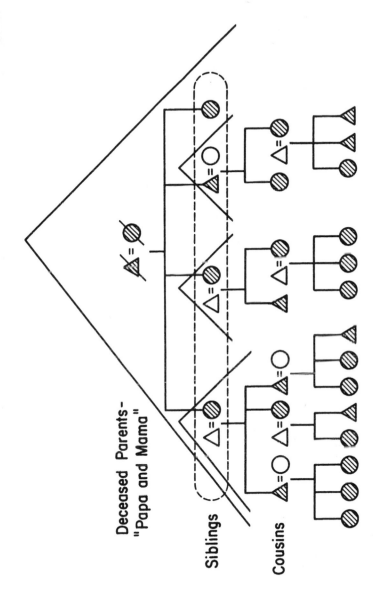

Figure 1. The cognatic descent group or "the greater family." Only shaded individuals are members of the family group. Spouses are not members of the family, but "in-laws."

tives. The descent group seen at the reunion is "ancestor focused," that is, it assembles because each person is a blood descendant of the same ancestral figure. Individuals bring their spouses to reunions, but spouses are not and can never be full members of the descent group itself.

The model of the cognatic descent group of the American South is one that fits neatly with the European form of family known as the "stem family," a form that predominated across the Saxon and Celtic lands from which these honored ancestors sprung. In the classic stem family, first labeled by LePlay (1884) and further described by Arensberg and Kimball (1940), only one son can inherit the land or the tenancy, and all the other children must either marry sons or daughters of nearby farmers or tenants, marry the daughter or son who is to inherit a shop in town, or travel to the city, where he or she would become a laborer or would, if clever and persistent, become educated to enter the church as a priest or a nun. This particular social organization of the family has been recognized as crucial in providing a socially fertile milieu in which the Industrial Revolution could take hold; there was a ready supply of labor for the growing towns and factories from peasant and farm tenanting families that were poised to send out their sons and daughters into the world to seek their fortunes. The nineteenth-century ancestor of the family who holds its reunions in the 1980s was one of the noninheritors who did not marry locally or go into the church—he traveled.

Historically, in the social form taken by this culturally constructed family, the process of "branching," or even "splitting" from the family tree was accomplished in America most often by migrating westward. Original arrivals of Scottish and Scotch-Irish people produced settlements in the early 1700s in Pennsylvania in the Susquehanna Valley; a new generation augmented by fresh arrivals trailed down into the Shenandoah; and another settled the Carolina Piedmont by 1790. The early nineteenth century saw splittings and movings out into former Indian territories of East Tennessee, North Georgia, and North Alabama and, finally, by the middle to late century, into Texas. The waves of migration are well documented in the literature of the settlement of the West and that of the history of the Protestant churches on the frontier.[2] The migrating group typically consisted of family clusters or sometimes two or three brothers with their wives and children or a small number of families who had been neighbors or members of the same congregation. They formed small farms in the new territory. Their community was one of scattered open-country neighborhoods centered on a rural church and/or graveyard. In a number of instances a common graveyard was set in the open countryside; in other cases the family buried its dead in a family plot in a field. Later, churches were built and families began to bring deceased members into the common cemetery alongside the church. Often, before a church was built, the community gathered for services under the trees with a traveling minister or, when there was no minister, simply for singing and praying and a shared meal. The linkages between familial and religious themes are so entwined that they are impossible to disentangle completely. A person became a founder of a church and a founder of a family by the same process—that of leaving home to seek ones fortune and eventually fulfilling the cultural prescription of being a successful, stalwart Protestant saint.

In the retelling of the story that surrounds the arrival and success of the founding ancestor of a family celebrating a reunion, the structure of the tale and its dramatic elements resemble the patterning of the tales that give legitimacy to various pilgrimage centers in Roman Catholicism, what the Turners call the *foundation narrative* of that center (Turner and Turner 1978:46–47). In this case the foundation narrative associated with reunions and with church homecomings is one in which a pioneer or a set of pioneers overcomes dangers and obstacles to make his way into a new land and subdue the forces of nature to create a rational, orderly, "civilized" society out of the wilderness. The ingredients of the "wilderness" include the natural elements—storms, snow, parching heat, drought, and floods. Also a part of the wilderness are the natural flora and fauna that had to be overpowered—the thickets to be cleared for fields, the prairies to be broken up with only the hand or ox-drawn plow, trees to be cut down to build houses and barns, wolves and coyotes to be killed to protect the livestock, rattlesnakes to be done away with, as well as numerous other predators of the particular region being settled, such as bears, bobcats, mountain lions, and scorpions. An especially powerful dramatic element in the narrative is introduced with the presence of the Indians,

always lurking just behind the trees or on the other side of the hill, a
force as feared and as romantically treated as other members of the
"natural world" of the wilderness, as a symbol of the powers of
darkness waiting to be overcome by the powers of light embodied
in civilization.[3]

In the drama of the story told about the ancestor and in the
drama of the reunion itself as a social form, history is being retold as
its recipients would like it to be. As in the parade in Yankee City
for the town's tercentenary celebration, where only a specific
number of incidents could be selected to be depicted on the floats
(Warner 1961:96), as in thousands of other social dramas that are
played out in ceremonial settings daily, only a specific number of
historical events can be portrayed in story, song, and general tradition. The histories of the families include the illustrious ancestors
that conform to the cultural image of Protestant sainthood. Those
who do not conform to this image are forgotten, or they become
bad examples, examples of what many families call "black sheep."
The reunion celebrates success. Those who were eaten by bears or
wolves did not become enshrined as ancestors, and those who
succumbed to nature by living with the Indians on a permanent
basis just as surely removed themselves from the competition.

The requirement to leave one's home in order to go out and
become successful as an individual is deeply embedded in the Protestant value system. This compelling drive to achieve and to become distinctive as a separate person fueled the industrial society of
Britain and Northern Europe and sent the early colonists into the
American continent. The individual leaving his or her family at the
same time cuts ties with the parents in order to form the new family
of the next generation, a family that must, of necessity, be willing
to move itself in response to the challenges of the expanding economy or the lure of the frontier.

In discussing this interplay of family symbolism with social
expression, W. Lloyd Warner writes the following of the Protestant imperative to leave one's family nest.

> In feudal society the family functioned to fix permanently the place of
> the individual. He was born to, and stayed in, one closed position. The
> fluid Renaissance, Protestant, and industrial societies, all terms for the
> several aspects of one basic change, emphasized the movement of free
> individuals and openness of status. The Puritans who came to Yankee

City to improve their *economic* and *religious* status also came to improve their *social* position. All were integral parts of a systematic change from an old to a new system. Birth into a family of a given status no longer fixed the entire career of the individual or all of his activities within the status. He was freer to do what he might to be master of his fate. He could move. (Warner 1961:80)

The reunion reunites a transgenerational set of families who, in following their cultural imperatives and playing out the roles required of them, cannot possibly remain together. They must, in other words, move in order to fulfill their calling as persons. This fissioning of units in every generation creates a ragged edge of relationships and a set of unresolved contradictions in loyalty. The loyalty to the new family of one's own procreation conflicts with the loyalty to the old family of one's birth; following the cultural prescription to seek one's fortune conflicts with the prescription to love and honor one's father and mother; the ideals of life in a small, comfortable, rural community conflicts with the ideals of becoming an individual success in the rational world of business and urban industry. The reunion as an annual ritual enables those who have scattered to be back together again. It enables those who give homage to the ideals of success and individual achievement to pause and give homage to the virtues of staying behind in tight-knit fellowship. And it validates the individual pilgrim journey through identification of honored ancestors who also left their homes and families "to seek a better life." It heals the cleavages while also prescribing additional tears in the fabric of the family.

The complex of gatherings constituting Protestant pilgrimage gives full social expression to the twin themes of individualism and corporateness that are so deeply embedded in Western Christianity. In the secular world surrounding the medieval church the predominant social unit was the family and the local village or urban neighborhood. In the village of rural Europe and Britain the individual was enmeshed in a web of descent and filiation tied to landholding and to the feudal system. Urban life had its own crosscutting group obligations based in kinship, local citizenship, and trade guild membership or apprenticeship. And for both the rural and urban person the most precious loyalty and set of obligations was to the corporate entity of the Holy Church, constructed of layers of hierarchies and overlapping sets of sacred personalities with their own demands on the piety of the person. The corporate and hierarchical forms of social relationships permeated one's structured world; pilgrimage provided the opportunity for expression of the counterpoint of that world in antistructural individuation on the pilgrim way. In the modern world of Protestant America, in contrast, the individual is expected to live out life as a unit apart, a pilgrim on a journey every day through the labyrinth of a legal-rational social universe, seeking one's fortune alone, exemplifying the virtues of ingenuity, thrift, hard work, and fulfilling one's destiny in a most personalized way. The "structure" in this world is the structure of the rational-technical world of work, where people are hired, transferred, moved, promoted, and dismissed on their own individual merit or lack of it, and where they are conceived in, socialized by, and launched from ideal nucleated household units with only fragile ties to extended kin. In this setting the antistructure is quite the opposite from the liminality of the personal pilgrim journey (for this is now the motif of daily life). It is the antistructure of obligation to a large family unit and a citizenship in a sacred locale, a place to call home. Its social expression, then, is in reunion, the reuniting of the wandering individuals, and in homecoming, the returning to a place from which they or their ancestors have gone away.

These twin themes of individuality and corporateness find expression not only in the reunion-homecoming configuration but also in other aspects of American Protestant symbolic life. In the heroic literature of nineteenth-century industrialism epitomized in the Horatio Alger stories, we find the contrastive but complementary hero types of the corporation-style hard worker and the creative entrepreneur. The first appears as the boy who makes good by working his way up from the mailroom of the big company to become its president, a paragon of corporate cooperation and endurance. The second is the boy who arrives penniless on the landscape of industrial America and, through his own cunning and skill, invents, combines, discovers, or in some way creates his own business success. Additional expressions of individual versus corporate models in the American novel include psychological sagas of the individual in conflict between the poles of self and society. These include stories of the individual searching for his or her "self" or identity, stories of rebellion, of family struggle between individuals and possessive parents, of struggles by persons seeking to "make it" in spite of family background, of adult lives marked by childhood conflict with mother or father, of the drive for self-fulfillment conflicting with the drive to fulfill one's social obligations. The literature of psychology and psychiatry portrays these images in scientific fashion, alternating between the advocacy of personhood achieved through individual actualization and personhood discovered through acquiescence to the demands of society. Sociological writings have expressed the same intellectual ambivalence. Community (symbolizing corporate life) is delineated as the antithesis of modern society (symbolizing anomie and individual rootlessness); rural is created as an ideal foil against urban; urban neighborhood life is discovered as an answer to the charge of urban noncommunity; and the journals of family sociology are replete with articles arguing whether the nuclear family exists or does not exist and whether the American family is dying.[4] Our national rhetoric itself is couched in this kind of language, and our politicians give evidence of these same recurring themes. Individuality is advocated for the integrity of every person, created equal and endowed with certain rights. Yet social responsibility and communal involvement are championed as crucial to the American dream.

A pattern is seen in the reunion-homecoming complex that is a part of a much larger pattern in Western Protestantism, especially in the Protestantism of the United States. This country was created through the process of leaving home. It advocates freedom as its hallmark. However, for millions of Americans, the Protestant version of pilgrimage offers the liminality of communitas and at the same time provides a metasocial commentary on their lives and on their experience. We see in the assemblages of individuals in the rural churchyards of the South in summertime a paradigmatic event in which overarching cultural meanings are explored and dramatized, in which a Protestant story is told and retold.

Women and Men

In the discussion of the social structure and organization of the family system of the white Protestant South, I have emphasized the notion of cognatic descent, with equal inheritance and kinship of male and female siblings. Within this system, however, there exists a pronounced matrilineal tendency. Furthermore, the role played by women in the outdoor ceremonial life is one of ritual specialist, the folk liturgist, the priestess of the outdoor church-family complex. The role of the woman as mother in the family and as central figure in the ceremonies associated with Protestant religious familism are aspects of the symbolic expression of the meanings of a culture in which women have a marginal, thus liminal, position in the rational, technical world of ordered social structure. They are placed by culture in an ambiguous situation. They are at one time part of the natural world—through their biological reality as those who give birth to children—and yet are necessary for the ongoing task of civilization, the subjugation of the natural by the cultural. This culturally ambiguous place is expressed here in the social relationships and social position of the woman in the cognatic descent group and, further, in the set of sacred symbols surrounding "mother" and "family" within the reunion and other gatherings.

The matrilineal tendency in Southern kinship is exemplified in several lines of evidence collected in my twelve-year study of Southern Presbyterians. The first line of evidence is that of patterns of attendance at family reunions: families in the current generation and in the grandparent one attend the reunion of the woman's family with far greater regularity and sense of obligation than that of the husband's family. If the husband's reunion is the preferred one for attendance, it is frequently the reunion of his mother's side of the family. And, if the family attends reunion of both sides, they are most likely to drop attendance at the father's family reunion after his death and continue to affiliate with that of the mother, even after her demise. A second line of evidence comes from the tendency of sisters to retain very close ties through summer visiting at their childhood home, bringing along their own small children for the visit with their mother. This visit may, but does not necessarily, coincide with the week of reunion; it may also be accompanied by periods of time when the cousins who are children of these sisters all visit grandmother's house together in the summer, especially if grandmother still lives in the country or lives near the site of the reunion. Meanwhile, the cousins of the same family whose fathers are brothers will be visiting at several different homeplaces with their own mothers and will therefore not develop the close associational and ceremonial ties of the children of sisters. Still a third bit of convincing data presents itself in linguistic clues coming from the process of labeling siblings who are born of remarried parents. Those who are born of the same mother but who have different fathers are consistently labeled "sister" and "brother." Children who are born of different mothers but who have the same father are, in contrast, labeled "half-sister" and "half-brother." This recognition of closer maternal relationship was borne out in actual practice in the previous generations by sending a young child or children to be reared by the mother's mother when the child's mother had died. If, on the other hand, a father died, the children were most certainly not sent away but remained with their widowed mother if at all possible, as one family unit for better or for worse.

The images of the mother in Southern Protestantism and in the literature of the Protestant frontier of early America are images of a beloved and faithful woman who has toiled for her family, given birth to many children, and watched them leave home one by one. She is idealized in nineteenth-century literature in the same way that the "community" is idealized—both are images of worlds that have been lost. The personal pain of mothers who have to part with their children and be alone in old age is no doubt related to the active role of mothers in the organization and continuation of the reunions of these same children and of their own siblings who have been motivated to "travel" in the fulfillment of the cultural prescriptions. Kimball and McClellan have caught the essence of the mother's story in the following quote from a personal history of a late nineteenth-century woman caught in the American Protestant dilemma.

One morning—it was the fifth of May 1888—he went away. He was just a little past eighteen years old—my last baby. I stood at the door to watch him go down the street. I cannot *tell* you how I felt. It was a lovely spring morning, but I felt as if the end of the world had come. No children in my home any more! The last going from me. Oh, Oh, Oh! And yet, I would not have held him back!

(Brown 1929:214, quoted in Kimball
and McClellan 1962:341)

The mother in American Protestant culture is a figure associated with the warmth of home, family, and *communitas*, that feeling of well-being generated by participation in ritual. When the reunions are seen as an expression of *communitas* (the soft, human side of an otherwise mechanized, inhuman urban world), it is not surprising to find the mother as a central figure in the reunion complex. The Protestant family here is played out in its most idealized form—the Reformed version of the holy family, with mother as human family leader and nurturer in place of Mary, the blessed but unreachable Virgin mother of the Holy Family in traditional Roman Catholic pilgrimage. The mother of Protestantism is the mother at the door, weeping and waving her hand as successive sons and daughters leave the nest to take their individual places in the world. She is the mother beside the hearth or in the modern kitchen preserving the tradition for those who periodically return from their wanderings. In the reunion she is the mother who gathers in her scattered flock of children and grandchildren for a return to the ideal world of rural life, natural setting, and loving community, and in this sacralized setting she is the priestess. She handles and presents the sacred elements of food and communion on the long tables under the trees. She is the liturgist in the ritual enactment of this tightly knit set of symbols and meanings known as the family reunion.

The warm, comfortable world of the family contrasts starkly with the rational technical world of town and city life, where the Protestant on the solitary journey must subdue the natural impulses of emotion and affect to the requirements of a pragmatic and controlled life in which the dominant images are those of time clocks, calendars, lists, responsibilities, contracts, legalities, and obligations. Emotion and affect have no place in the controlled, ordered life. Modern bureaucratic life is, in fact, a cultural image associated with males and "male reasoning," the thought process of the rational-technical bureaucracy. Males have been the primary inhabitants of this outside world, the world of the ordered corporation, the bureaucracies of industry and of the professions. Women, on the other hand, are associated in this cultural construct with the inside world, the natural emotional side of humanity, with the images of birth and life, of milk and human kindness, of blood and vitality, of death and of weakness. These are the uncontrollables—

the power of feeling and the power of life-giving—and as such are revered and feared. Because of their position as inhabitants of the revered and feared side of the cultural world, women are in this Protestant universe the marginal dwellers, attaining almost magical status as holders of "intuition" and "woman's touch."

The organization of the ideal world of men and women in Southern Protestant Christianity might be compared to the separation of inside/outside of the house in Berber culture, as seen by Bordieu, especially the Berber view of the sexual division of labor and of sexual meanings. He describes the Berber house as follows.

> Considered in its relationship with the external world, which is a specifically masculine world of public life and agricultural work, the house, which is the universe of women and the world of intimacy and privacy, is *haram*, that is to say, at once sacred and illicit for every man who does not form part of it. . . .   (Bordieu 1973:102)

In the symbolic universe of Southern Protestantism, the woman belongs to the house and the man to the public, outside world of business and industry. The woman is the cultural specialist in all things connected to the house and its operation. She is also in charge of the children, food, celebration of family birthdays, holidays, and vacations, and she is the specialist for ritual. Her ritual specialty is not that of the public, secular world but of the private, personal, sacred world of family. She knows all the rules for holding weddings, bride's parties, teas and coffees, church fund-raising events, Thanksgiving, Christmas, and family reunion.

The reunion activities are an extension of the role of woman as keeper of the Protestant house and custodian of the religious culture that is to be passed on to the children through ritual occasions. The fact that many women who attend reunions also hold jobs outside the home in no way affects the overall structure of this double universe, for the traditional role of woman is to be the keeper of the house and of the children in addition to whatever other economic role she may hold. Therefore, the woman who works outside the home is also expected to work inside the home and to be responsible for its organization and management. The husband is expected to "help" his wife with household tasks, but she is in charge and must answer for the final result.

The mother in her role as cultural specialist has the responsibility of carrying on and transmitting the heritage in much the same way as the mother in Jewish culture. In each of these cases the assignment of the woman to the crucial task of ritual celebration in the home and within the family sphere at the same time has removed her, until quite recently, from officiating at public rituals in the formal church and synagogue services. In Southern Presbyterian tradition, for example, it was impossible for women to serve as elders until the middle 1960s, which meant that they were disallowed from handling the elements of Communion and of participating in the Sacrament of Baptism. Women could not be ordained as ministers in the church until recent years, which barred them from preaching in the official capacity of teaching elder, interpreter of the scriptures, the central feature of Presbyterian public worship. Women, therefore, in the Presbyterianism of the Southern United States—and also in Methodist and Baptist churches—have been relegated to passive participants in the formal, public worship services and have been assigned active, organizational roles in the informal, private world of family-religious ritual.

One public, ceremonial role in the reunion is reserved for the men—the "saying of the blessing" at the beginning of the meal itself, usually while everyone is lined up at the tables waiting to begin to fill their plates. The person selected for this task is often the eldest male in the ancestral line being honored; it might be a male who has "married into the family" if that person is elderly and revered or if he is an ordained minister. One other variation occurs in the female/male division of labor. On the evening before the reunion in some families, men barbecue meat or cook hamburgers on the charcoal grill for the early comers; in some gatherings the barbecued meat becomes the main dish of the reunion food, but it is always supplemented by other foods traditionally prepared by the women. In recent years families have been known to have catered meals or to hold their reunions inside a community center or church hall, in which cases the female/male roles are again blurred. In the outdoor gatherings, however, the women traditionally hold the ritual roles of producer, director, and stage manager in the drama of the reunion. They are, in fact, the outdoor liturgists.

The role of women as outdoor liturgists in the providing and officiating at reunions presents a reversal of their traditional role as inactive spectators in the formal services of established denominational worship. The significance of this reversal is seen even more clearly when viewed as one aspect of the overall pattern of reversal in the commensal meal itself, a symbolic encapsulation of Protestant culture. The Eucharist in the medieval church and the contemporary Roman Catholic Church presents in capsulized form the core meanings of the universe of that religious world. The communion theme is crucial in the reunion in knitting together the scattered family and providing a symbolic center of annual gathering.

The Communion of the Saints

Food and commensality have long been viewed by anthropologists as deeply symbolic of human group solidarity, especially in the marking of boundaries of kinship or ethnic affiliation. In Christian tradition the partaking of the Sacrament of the Lord's Supper has held center stage in this commensal symbolism. I contend that the same symbolic importance attaches to the outdoor celebration of partaking of a joint meal—that coparticipation in the reunion food symbolizes membership in the body of the family of faith, just as participation in the indoor Communion symbolizes membership in the body of Christ, or the formally organized church.

In her study of food symbolism in Judaic-Christian tradition, Gillian Feeley-Harnick treats food as a language, serving as the medium through which messages were conveyed concerning God and his creation (Feeley-Harnick 1981). She notes that in both the Old and New Testaments there is a rich symbolism associated with food and commensality. Bread becomes a metaphor for eternal life, for obedience, for the Word of God, and commensality, she argues, is a metaphor for the covenant people. She says "The consequence of eating God's words is the covenant, 'the creator of all rights and duties' in Judaism. . ." (Feeley-Harnick 1981:11). Commensality, she states, is a powerful marker in the definition of kinship and of group affiliation in the Bible and also in the extensive literature from anthropology.

> Commensality, expressed in ordinary meals or wedding feasts or commemorative meals like the jaBirisi ceremony among the Gururumba of New Guinea (Newman 1965) or the passover and eucharist . . . can be

understood only in terms of interrelated cultural systems and associated behavior. . . . In establishing precisely who eats what with whom, commensality is one of the most powerful ways of defining and differentiating social groups.   (Feeley-Harnick 1981:11)

Those who eat together at a family reunion eat certain special categories of food. One learns from years of experience that the correct ceremonial foods for a reunion include fried chicken, ham, vegetable casseroles, potato salad, gelatin salad, chopped marinated vegetable salad, deviled eggs, relish trays, and certain special pies and cakes. While these may have originally been functional foods, popular items in the country, or easily affordable foods in Depression times, they are in the 1980s not necessarily easy, popular, or affordable. They are instead, symbolic. They are carefully prepared by each mother and presented as her own contribution to the whole. They are consumed primarily by others. One does not ordinarily eat only one's own reunion food but samples the dishes brought by everyone else. The sharing of food prepared by others is highly symbolic in the expression of oneness as the family.[5] In this instance, the reunion meal becomes a sacred meal, a form of celebrating communion.

The Roman Catholic sacred meal is the Eucharist; its inverse Protestant one is the outdoor communion. In his discussion of symbols of the Eucharist, Firth points out that "the Eucharistic ideas of a communion obtained by partaking of the bodily substance of the god are in conformity with a wide range of symbolic concepts which unite sacred with secular in food, as it is consumed" (Firth 1973:425; cf. Fortes 1966b:21). Firth goes on to say that "They belong too to that sector of concepts in which it is not the food which becomes sanctified, but the sanctified which becomes food." In the case of the Roman Catholic tradition, the body and blood of Christ become food for the Eucharist in the transformation of the everyday elements of bread and wine. In the case of the family reunion and other Protestant outdoor ceremonial meals, the assembled body of Christ as the priesthood of believers is shared together and the sanctified community becomes food at the hands of those who prepared it. The body of Christ is the food of the community, the shared elements of ordinary food at this time transformed into special food for a special symbolic ceremony.

Unlike the Mass or the indoor celebration of Holy Communion in Protestantism, the reunion has no spoken liturgy, no Book of Church Order or prayer book to guide its liturgists in the celebration of the sacrament. The words that are said over the meal as a blessing are ordinary words of thanks and of petition for the safety and health of the assembled kin group. The absence of or sparsity of verbal ordering and written text to accompany deeply engrained ritual has been studied by anthropologists for nonindustrial societies, and the insights gained there have been applied to certain ritual practices and occasions in our own industrial, Western society. In her analysis of symbolic behavior cross culturally, Mary Douglas, following Bernstein (1971), refers to the use of the "restricted code" of condensed symbols. In this type of performance, ritual, or day-to-day behavior, few words are used; instead, the message is communicated by being encoded in the sequence and order of persons, space, food, and other culturally selected paraphernalia. She notes as an example of this restricted code the specified obligatory distribution of certain parts of an animal in hunting and gathering peoples to certain categories of kin and also the distribution of first fruits in an agricultural feast. Here, she says, the social order is expressed in the condensed symbols of the ritual feast. In applying these insights to British and American family ritual, Douglas states the following

> Clearly the words which accompany these distributions carry a small part only of the significance of the occasion. The comparable situations in family life would be the spatial layout of chairs in the living room which convey the hierarchy of rank and sex, the celebration of Sunday dinner, and for some families, presumably those in which a restricted code is used, every meal and every rising, bathing and bed-time is structured to express and support the social order. Bernstein's fully personal family, then, would be one in which no meals were taken in common and no hierarchy recognized, but in which the mother would attempt to meet the unique needs of each child by creating an entirely individual environment of time-table and services around each one of her brood; . . .   (Douglas 1973:55)

Clearly, the Protestant family in day-to-day urban or town life falls somewhere between Douglas' two extremes of formality in terms of its systems of encoded messages. However, in a regular school

year the family life of reunion goers is often geared partly to the
schedules of each person, especially to those of each child. In the
reunion, meanwhile, the order is set and repetitive, communicating
the hierarchy of office from old to young, from ancestor to descendants, and placing women and men in their fixed traditional
positions that may not correspond with their roles in the rational-
technical, secular universe.

In the secular world of the city, the liturgist is the public
figure, the man. However, in contrast to the indoor church service,
where the elements of bread and wine are handled and dispensed
only by the ordained priest or minister, a man, in the outdoor
church, the reunion food is handled and dispensed by the women.
The roles of women and men are inverted. The woman's position
of marginality to the secular world is reversed. She is central in the
reunion.

The position of the Protestant extended family reunited in
sacred time provides a clear example of Victor Turner's idea of
liminality as one of the locations for true communitas to take place.
Turner notes that commensality, or dining together, is often a
symbol of communitas in pilgrimage. It is also true for Turner that
liminality, or communitas, is always expressed within a particular
cultural idiom. He notes this culture-specific notion as follows.

> though pilgrimages strain in the direction of universal communitas, they
> are still ultimately bounded by the structure of the religious systems
> within which they are generated and persist.   (Turner 1974:205)

It is thus that the pilgrimages of the medieval church and of European Roman Catholicism express the communitas of a Eucharistic
experience of the pilgrims that is focused on meanings of the
sharing of the sacrament that are completely different from the
meanings of this sharing when engaged in by Protestants. In Chapter Two I emphasized this contrast as it takes shape in the outdoor
Communion service as compared to the celebration of the Eucharist
in the Mass, which I called the "indoor church." This contrast can
be carried further to contrast the entire complex of commensality
within Protestantism, including both the indoor Communion and
the outdoor food sharing I have described for reunions, with that of
the Roman Catholic ecclesiastical commensality. The first is cen-

tered on the food as symbolic of the communion of the saints assembled; the second is centered on the Eucharist as the presence of Christ's body and blood.

In his study of the shape and pattern of Catholic liturgy over the centuries, Dix (1945) finds that a continuous structure of the celebration of the Eucharist persists. Liturgy, as used by Dix, refers to "the act of taking part in the solemn corporate worship of God by the 'priestly' society of Christians, who are 'the Body of Christ, the church.'" He states:

> In the course of time the term "The Liturgy" has come to be particularly applied to the performance of that rite which was instituted by our Lord Jesus Christ Himself to be the peculiar and distinctive worship of those who should be "His own;" and which has ever since been the heart and core of Christian worship and Christian living—the Eucharist or Breaking of Bread. (Dix 1945:1)

He goes on to explain further.

> By the time the New Testament came to be written the Eucharist already illuminated everything concerning Jesus for His disciples—His Person, His Messianic office, His miracles, His death, and the redemption that He brought. It was the vehicle of the gift of His Spirit, the means of eternal life, the cause of the unity of His church.
> (Dix 1945:4)

The metaphor of the Eucharist for the Roman Catholic is a metaphor of social intercourse between Jesus and the individual, "the familiar intercourse of Jesus abiding in the soul, as a friend who enters and sups with a friend" (Dix 1945:4).

The entry of Jesus into the soul of the communicant is predicated on the theological interpretation of the transformation of the everyday substances of bread and wine into the actual body and blood of Jesus. This doctrine was one of the most pronounced markers between Reformers and the traditional church. The doctrine is one of magical and mystical activity, which was thrown out by the Reformers, along with the mystical powers of the saints to appear or intercede and the mystical powers of healing waters, relics, or artifacts, all associated with pilgrimage. On the subject of the central place of the doctrine of transubstantiation in Roman Catholic theology, Mary Douglas has the following comment.

> Symbolizing does not exhaust the meaning of the Eucharist. Its full
> meaning involves magical or sacramental efficacy. If it were just a matter
> of expressing all these themes, symbolizing and commemorating, much
> less blood and ink would have been spilt at the Reformation.
>
> (Douglas 1973:70)

The Reformers objected to the magic powers of the Mass as
sacrifice, or as a "work," an instrument of arriving at salvation. To
the Reformer the Lord's Supper was a sign and a promise, but not
an end in itself. Even the words used to denote the celebration of
the sacrament indicate something of the way in which the two
traditions continue to view the rite. While the Roman Catholic
word is Eucharist or, more generally, the Mass or the Liturgy, the
Protestants invariably use the word Communion or Lord's Supper.
In Methodist writings the latter designation is found more often,
perhaps because of the connection early Methodists made to the
agape meals of fellowship from the early church.[6]

Both Methodists and Presbyterians hold to the institutionalized orders for communion in the ongoing tradition of the denominations, the seminaries, and the calendar of the "indoor church."
Communion is celebrated within the church service on the first
Sunday of every quarter in most Presbyterian churches. In Methodism a running debate continues within theology faculties and
among ministers and their congregations over the appropriateness
of more frequent communion; those advocating greater frequency
are accused of being "high church" by those whose rural moorings
predispose them to favor the less frequent schedule.

Mary Douglas argues in her treatment of the Mass and the
Eucharist in *Natural Symbols* that the persons who are socialized in
what she designates "grid-like" socially tight-knit communities
respond to the tight, complex body of mystery and magic encoded
in the Mass. Meanwhile, those do *not* who are those socialized in
highly "personal" or isolated nuclear families with heavy emphasis
on verbalization and rational explanation (Douglas 1973:70). This
interpretation of the social patterns that underlie ritual participation
and the formation of metaphor is congruent with the data on
Protestant pilgrimages in reunions and homecomings. Those people who are verbal, rational, and capitalistic in their lifeways are
also those who view their lives as individual pilgrimages and who
are free to move away from family and kin in order to achieve their

personal goals. These are the people whose pilgrimage I have attempted to document and to subject to some tentative explanations.

The absence of any written text for any of these outdoor family and religious gatherings does not mean that their programming is not repetitive and almost completely predictable in its recurrent order from time to time. What it does mean is that these gatherings represent a tradition that is not a part of the written "high church" code that Redfield (1941) would have called the Great Tradition. Instead, these gatherings fall into Redfield's Little Tradition, or folk tradition, in that their rules for performance are carried in the heads of the participants and transmitted orally and through example to the following generations. In attempting to unravel this aspect of coded behavior in ritual. I have called on the linguistic work of Basil Bernstein, who holds that speech forms (and, correspondingly for Douglas' extension of this argument, behavioral forms) fall into two types of behavioral codes: *restricted* codes for informal, in-group communication and *elaborated* codes for public, formal, written, and oratorical communication.[7] While Bernstein's analysis applies to the relationship between speech and behavioral forms and social class, Douglas applies the notion to the "levels of complexity" in society. For example, bands and tribes would be expected to engage more extensively in the restricted codes, and urban complex societies would be expected to engage more in elaborated codes (Douglas 1973). The same would hold true of ritual. However, in those arenas within urban society where one finds Turner's liminality, the communitas of the pilgrimage, for instance, one would expect to find more use of the restricted codes than the elaborated ones. In the case of the reunion, the restricted code comes into play within a ritual process that is a part of the annual cycle of a people who also engage in highly elaborated behavioral and ritual codes during their lives in town and urban situations. Each one conveys a different sort of information and is suited to a different kind of social order. The social order of the reunion is that of a liminal time, a sacred place, and a symbolic order that states Protestantism for Protestants in the same way that pilgrimages to saints' shrines states Catholicism for Catholics.

In analyzing the way these symbolic codes operate within the processes of communitas or antistructure, Turner gives the follow-

ing account of the transmission of culture within the tribal initiation
and also within liminal phases of complex societies, phases he calls
"passages, margins, and poverty," all of which he associates with
pilgrimage.

> Often, but not always, myths are recited explaining the origin, attri-
> butes, and behavior of these strange and sacred inhabitants of liminality.
> Again, sacred objects may be shown to the novices. . . . These symbols,
> visual and auditory, operate culturally as mnemonics, or as communica-
> tions engineers would no doubt have it, as "storage bins" of informa-
> tion, not about pragmatic techniques, but about cosmologies, values,
> and cultural axioms whereby a society's deep knowledge is transmitted
> from one generation to another. Such a device, in the setting of "a place
> that is not a place, and a time that is not a time" (as the Welsh folklorist
> and sociologist Alwyn Rees once described for me the context of Celtic
> bardic utterance), is all the more necessary in cultures without writing,
> where the whole cultural deposit has to be transmitted either through
> speech or by repeated observation of standardized behavioral patterns
> and artifacts.   (Turner 1974:239)

In the reunion complex we have a culture with writing, to be
sure, but one in which the writing dominates secular individualized
Protestant culture and in which informal oral tradition is strong in
the reunion of the community of believers. Both are important
aspects of this culture's overall pattern of organization. Within the
rituals of reunion, the inner world of culture can be given full
expression.

In the family reunion we see a statement about the family in
Protestant culture, as it is conceptualized and as it "should be." We
see this statement being made in the language of food, activities,
rhythms, intensities of action, roles of women and men, and the
arrangement of symbolic materials—rural homeplaces, tables in the
churchyard, pictures and stories of the ancestors. A second style of
gathering brings together a number of families into an association
or an extended network in an honored sacred place—a certain
cemetery, a church, or a traditional camp meeting ground. The
gatherings held at these places bring together associated families
and resemble a sort of joint family reunion in form and content.
They are enacting variations on the themes of the ongoing drama
of Protestant life in urban society. They become a second type of
Protestant pilgrimage.

CHAPTER FOUR

The Sacred Place—Cemetery, Church, Camp Meeting Ground

IN A SOCIETY where mobility is the rule and individuals find themselves propelled away from their families into personal lives aimed at fulfillment and achievement, it is not surprising that one of the objects of nostalgia is the permanent fixed place, the location to which one might return "home" for a time in order to become refreshed. Few American Protestants, in fact, have such a permanent home base. Their own parents have moved about in response to job opportunities, corporate demands, personal ambitions, or preference for different locations, and their grandparents were the children either of immigrants or of pioneers. Sacred places form the focus for summer pilgrimages by Protestants in the shape of cemetery or church homecomings and camp meetings at rural campgrounds.

The Cemetery Association Day

Just as the Worthy family will gather in honor of a common ancestor each June, so the Martin's Crossing Cemetery Association will hold a homecoming. On the Sunday morning of the homecoming the older men of the association arrive early and start cooking barbecued chicken for the main course of the noon meal. Later the women will arrive with various dishes of family reunion-style picnic food. Couples with young children will come later, too, as will those who have driven for several hours to reach the cemetery.

The gathering assembles under a tin-roofed shed with open sides, built over a concrete slab. Folding chairs fill the arbor, and a portable lectern rests at the front of the congregation. Under this roof the morning service will be held, beginning with a welcome from the association president and prayers given by one of the members, followed by the singing of old favorite hymns, led by an appointed song leader.

The arriving couples and their children have been strolling around the cemetery before wandering slowly into the arbor for the morning services. The sounds of the singing call the last remaining clusters of people away from their systematic visits to the graves of their ancestors. As he stands thoughtfully gazing at a grave marked by one of the earliest headstones, Richard Wilkins begins to speak softly to explain his attachment to this pleasant place, nestled in a grove of trees, settled on a rolling hillside near the river. He tells the following story.

> This is my great-grandfather, Daniel Wilkins, who was one of the original settlers in this area. He came in a wagon train with his four brothers to Texas in 1848 from East Tennessee and started farms right here along the river. They were some of the first white settlers in these parts, and they had a tough go of it. And this is my great-grandmother. She was Elizabeth Haynes. So the Haynes and the Wilkins are the two largest families here. Over there is the Haynes family plot. Her father came into the county some time after 1848, and she married my grandfather then. See old Mr. Hamilton over there looking at that grave? Well, that's his grandfather—Samuel Haynes, who was the brother to my great-grandmother. Oh, this place is filled up with Haynes and Wilkins and their children.
>
> I was born in that house over there in 1909, and I lived there until I was about thirteen years old. Then my grandfather died and my father and his brothers decided to split up the land, and he sold his part and bought a ranch out in West Texas and we moved to that ranch then. But we always came back here to see my grandmother, and my dad always told us about growing up out here in the country. And now I never miss one of these get-togethers, because I like to see this place again and all these folks who are connected to my family.   (traditional narrative)

As he walks over to the arbor for the service, Richard Haynes is remembering the past; the devotional talk given by one of his cousins reinforces that meditation. The speaker has chosen for his topic "The Faith of Our Fathers." He speaks of the faith it required of the original forebearers to leave the settled homes of Tennessee and come to this land "to make a better life for themselves and for their children." He speaks of the faith of the people who built up the farms and the towns that surround the little cemetery in a corridor of growth that is rapidly becoming an urban area. He speaks of the family historians who have recorded all the ancestors and their accomplishments. He uses these illustrations as examples of how the living descendants should order their own lives in dedication to difficult tasks and in reliance on Jesus.

As the service draws to a close, the activity shifts to the tables nearby, wooden planks set on trestles and covered with white paper. Women begin to uncover their food, the barbecued chickens appear in large pans, the iced tea containers are set on the drink table, and the announcement is made for the elderly and those with young children to begin the line after the blessing has been said. The line moves slowly down the table, and families congregate to eat their lunch and to talk about the news, the beautiful day, or about the business meeting that will decide about the new fence for the cemetery and the trees that should be cut down. After lunch the business meeting is held in the same arbor where a few hours earlier the religious services had taken place.

The meeting of the Martin's Crossing Cemetery Association is called to order each year only one time, on the first Sunday in June. The current president asks for the minutes of the previous year's meeting. The officers are cousins and friends. The meeting is chatty and anecdotal. This year the case is made for a new fence around the cemetery, and the vote is unanimous to use some of the association funds to build the fence. The treasurer has reported a healthy balance in the bank, and several ideas are put forth regarding needed improvements on the grounds—an enlarged cooking area, an improved rest room, the removal of some dead trees. The tree removal carries the day, and another unanimous vote authorizes money to be spent for this endeavor. The membership list is discussed, and the announcement is made of the amount of annual dues to be paid by each family. The meeting is adjourned. Gradually, the assembly area is emptied of its inhabitants. The men who barbecued begin cleaning up. The women remove their covered dishes and picnic coolers from the tables; some young men and boys begin to take down the trestles and put away the tabletops for another year.

The act of coming together as an association dates back into the 1950s for the Martin's Crossing group, but other groups at other cemeteries have assembled since the turn of the century. The graves must be maintained, they say, and the cemetery must not be allowed to fall into ruin. In cultural terms, the ancestors must be given homage. The dead must be honored and the living must create ways of remembering.

The old cemetery at Liberty Hill has had an ongoing cemetery association since 1912, but the first official cemetery association day for this group, known in the town of Liberty Hill as "Homecoming," was held in 1953. A regional newspaper describes the gathering in this way:

> First Sunday in June 1953 is a day long to be remembered by Liberty Hill people as the first meeting of their homecoming organization. It was a successful day with large attendance, perfect weather, plenty to eat, preaching on the ground and the reunion of over 1,000 old friends. It has been decided to make this an annual affair and plans are made to incorporate under the name of Liberty Hill Memorial Homecoming Association.
>
> The association is to be non-profit for the purpose of financing permanent upkeep for the Liberty Hill Cemetery. It has been a custom in small communities to gather at the cemetery once a year and "clean the graveyard." Under such arrangements, cemeteries are not properly kept. . . .   (*Austin American-Statesman*,
>   Wednesday, June 10, 1953)

The Thirty-third Annual Memorial Homecoming was held on the first Sunday in June 1985; again, sunny weather, a large attendance, plenty to eat, and preaching on the grounds were all elements in the day's events. By 1985 the association had adopted the custom of having the noon meal catered by a popular local barbecue caterer, but the pattern of lining up by families and eating in clusters of extended kin remained firm. A tabernacle now covered the assembly area and a loudspeaker system carried the voice of the reader as she called out the names of all those who had died in the past year. And the association now had enough money accumulated in its bank accounts to keep the grass cut and the curbs trimmed and to make various improvements; but these matters were all deferred until the Annual Business Meeting on the third Sunday in October. At this homecoming one does not do business. One visits relatives and honors the dead.

Cemetery associations have foundation narratives similar to those of family reunions. Here the foundation narrative often refers to the settlement of this particular town or open-country neighborhood by a group of settlers, one of whom gave the land for the cemetery. In the case of Liberty Hill, the narrative goes this way:

> In 1852, when the early settlers of "old Liberty Hill" were beginning to establish their homes along the South San Gabriel River, members of another family were leaving their home in Greenville District, South Carolina, to begin the long trip to Texas. John T. Bryson, who was born in 1813 in Henderson County, North Carolina, with his wife Amelia Edwards Bryson, with six of their eight children (two were born in Texas) came to Gay Hill in Washington County to reside for a few months before moving on to Williamson County, where they built a house, still standing, on what came to be known as "Bryson Hill" near Old Liberty Hill. The house, built in 1854 of Bastrop County cedar, freighted in by ox wagon, was in the style of the day, with long front porch, dogrun, outside kitchen and smokehouse, all enclosed by a rock fence with stile and stone mounting block for the horseback riders.
>
> As more settlers moved in, the need for a community cemetery became apparent, and John T. Bryson met that need. As stated in the deed, "Due to my desire to secure for my family and for the people generally in this community, a permanent and properly improved Burial Ground," on 20 March, 1875, he signed a quit-claim deed to three and one half acres of his land, which deed was recorded in Williamson County on 11 August, 1875.
>
> (Fay Bryson Richardson 1970, quoted in Liberty Hill Cemetery Association 1984:41)

The mimeographed booklet published by the Liberty Hill Cemetery Association contains a complete listing of the burials and maps of the sections, with lot numbers coded to persons interred. This practice is one that is attempted by many of the small rural cemeteries, and the listing of all the burials in all the cemeteries in the county is a popular project for county historical societies. In the spring of 1985 such a project had reached near completion for Williamson County, Texas, due to the efforts and perseverance of a handful of women who had become specialists in local history and family genealogy. Searching for one's ancestors and constructing genealogies forms an important element in the reconstruction of the ideal cultural past and in the weaving of the stories that form the foundation narratives for each of the different types of reunions. Such a project serves, as do the cemetery gatherings, to honor the dead and to construct a set of cultural meanings for their descendants.

The dead form an important ingredient in the pilgrimages of Roman Catholicism, many of these being to shrines centered on the graves of martyrs or on the vision of someone having to do with the appearance of a holy figure who is dead. Beliefs about purgatory are also characteristic of Roman Catholic pilgrimages, a configuration of beliefs that, according to Turner, "have received most reinforcement from pre-Christian religious beliefs in the western fringes of Europe, in the surviving haunts of the Celtic peoples" (1975:122). Turner refers to the work of Christian in stating that "Devotion for and worry about the dead is characteristic of the entire Atlantic fringe from Galicia, through Brittany, Ireland, and England" (Turner 1975:94). This belief, which Turner ties to "Celtic animism," is also mentioned by Arensberg as a characteristic of the religious beliefs of his Atlantic Fringe communities, where old age is venerated in fairy and witch cults and where magical properties are assigned to sacred places in nature (Arensberg 1965). Turner also notes the transfer of Galacian and Asturian beliefs about the dead to unite with pre-Christian Aztec traditions in Mexico in the annual celebration of the Day of the Dead (Turner 1975:122). Gatherings in graveyards for honoring the dead and, in some cases, bringing food and flowers to graves are not unknown throughout Western Europe.[1]

The Protestant version of the veneration of old age and of the dead takes the form of the reverence for and respect of the founding ancestors, the original settlers and family heads. Again, the pause at the foot of the ancestor's grave to recite the narrative is the verbal homage and the transmission of the tradition to the younger family members who will listen.

The veneration of the ancestors also takes the form of keeping the grass and shrubs of the cemetery neatly manicured and maintaining the fences, tombstones, and grave plots in good repair. Additionally, the honor of the dead is expressed in decorating the graves with flowers. In his extensive survey of the space use and material culture of Texas graveyards, Jordan (1982) devotes several paragraphs to the custom of "working" the cemetery, which he connects to the gathering for Decoration Day. He describes the event in the following passage:

> The laborious job of scraping, as well as mounding and decoration, belong to the men, women and children alike. The women are also responsible for preparing a noon meal, served at the cemetery. Many rural graveyards are equipped with permanent, elongated serving tables to facilitate the noon meal, consisting of loose boards resting on saw-horses.   (Jordan 1982:29)

Because of his background and interest in cultural geography, Jordan ascribes the origin of many cemetery customs to the survival and diffusion of practices from Europe and Africa, such as the practice of leaving food on the graves for the dead or planting certain symbolic shrubs and flowers. He attributes the graveyard reunion to the early functional necessity of having people assemble to clean and scrape graves and plant grass and trees. An alternate explanation is that the customs associated with "working" the cemetery and planting trees and shrubs was an outgrowth of the reunion, itself a gathering in honor of the dead.

The dead and the living are intricately connected through the reunion at the Protestant cemetery. In the sense that here the dead are also relatives, family members, ancestors, and not just general "souls in purgatory," the reunion resembles more the role of the dead in tribal initiations observed by Turner. Of this relationship he says:

> In the liminality of initiations, the dead often appear as near or remote ancestors, connected by putative ties of consanguinity or affinity with the living, part of a communion of kin beginning with the founding ancestors, and hopefully, with due performance of ritual, continuing to the end of the world.   (Turner 1975:117)

In the Protestant rural cemetery one finds an almost total absence of iconography, another stark contrast to the pilgrim shrines of the Roman Catholic religious tradition. In keeping with the Calvinistic insistence on the removal of all vestiges of the elaborate symbolism of the medieval church, the outdoor expression of this cultural tradition is devoid of ornamentation except for an occasional simple cross. The tombstones are mostly plain, rectangular slabs of stone. The oldest ones are engraved with slogans or sayings and occasionally with a scroll or a garland of leaves. The newer ones are plain except for the names of the deceased and his or her birth and death dates. There are no statues of people in these cemeteries—not to the Virgin Mary, the saints, or even to the revered ancestors. The only cross may be found on a single gravestone or as a marker for a military grave.

In commenting on the distinctive traditions of Southern Protestant cemeteries, Wilson notes that:

> Southern cemeteries have generally not been sanctified ground, but they have reflected the region's religious outlook and its cultural differences from the North. . . . The country graveyards have the best claim to being identifiably regional institutions containing religious elements. . . . Family burial grounds have been especially noteworthy in Dixie, dating back to the pioneer times. Many rural congregations from the 19th century onward built their churches near these small family-burial plots and then extended them into larger church graveyards.
>
> (Wilson 1985:143)

Throughout the Southern United States today one sees this mixture of burial patterns: the open-country cemetery, where several interrelated families are buried, sometimes also members together of a now-lost congregation; the cemetery adjoining a rural church; and the civic or town cemetery, which sometimes was begun as the graveyard for an open-country crossroads community.

The Cemetery Association Day at one of these sacred places represents a gathering that is at once a kin-based and a religious event. The assembly of interrelated families has a transgenerational tie. They are products of related families who moved together, the offspring of the westward migration. They also have a tie in that they share the Protestant faith and the variation of Protestantism that values individual enterprise and personal achievement. The worship service and its devotional talk emphasize these individualistic themes, but with the tempering of family rootedness—the individual is rooted in a specific family and a specific location. The ancestors of those who went westward into Kentucky, Tennessee, North Alabama, and Texas were also pioneer Protestants from the

Carolinas whose own forebearers were originally from Scotland and from Ulster. The reunion rituals of all these people, of the culture and community patterns of which they are a part, include the same outdoor gathering, the honor of the deceased ancestors who are founders of families and churches, the reaffirmation of kin-group affiliation through shared food, the verbal seal of this affiliation in "the blessing" or, more formally, the devotional service, and the family meeting with its recognitions and introductions. Closely linked to the cemetery reunion but expressing the honor of a specific local congregation is the reunion known as church home-coming.

The Church Homecoming

The old Fairfield Presbyterian Church in the country in North Georgia is declining in membership and has a "supply preacher" from the seminary in Atlanta on the regular Sundays of the year; yet on the second Sunday in July, the congregation swells to several hundred worshippers. Church homecoming is a day when "all the sons and daughters of the congregation" can reassemble for preaching services and dinner on the grounds. The small sanctuary is filled to overflowing with people on this day. Bright summer flowers adorn the chancel. A special bulletin has been printed, detailing the order of service, giving the names of those who were the founders of the congregation, and providing information about the guest preacher, a former pastor of the church, who will deliver the homecoming sermon. The choir has prepared a special anthem for the occasion. During the service the minister takes the opportunity to thank "all those who have had a part in the preparations for this grand day." He also recognizes those who have "come from near and far to celebrate together this day in which we honor the church founders and those who have made possible this community of worship over the years." The guest minister is introduced; the sermon highlights the values of tradition and of faithfulness; the final hymn is followed by the benediction; and the congregation begins to turn and visit with old friends and cousins and the children of old friends. They gradually disperse, stopping to shake hands with the minister and the guest preacher, and then they take on their positions for the next event—the dinner on the grounds.

As in the family reunion and the cemetery reunion, the central feature of the church reunion or church homecoming is the communal meal. Again, the food has been prepared with great care by each mother. Again, it is laid out in prescribed order along the outdoor tables. Again, a blessing is said and the people pass along the tables in single file, serving their plates with the food prepared by their relatives and friends. Again, families sit together in small clusters to eat with their own children and grandchildren, and again they then move about to visit with their peers. Again, laughter can be heard over the meadows and fields as stories of bygone days are traded. Those who played together on adjoining farms and attended Sunday school and church together as children share their reminiscences and inquire politely about each other's lives away from the old community. In this particular gathering the attenders come primarily from the Atlanta area or that of larger North Georgia towns and cities. Homecoming will be celebrated here on this Sunday; it will be celebrated at hundreds of other country churches on other Sundays. Town churches will also announce "homecomings" patterned on those known from the country, with an especially elaborate celebration marking the fiftieth, one hundredth, and one hundred twenty-fifth anniversaries.

While the focal point of the family reunion is the common ancestor from whom all those present are descended and the focal point of the cemetery reunion is the set of pioneers who came into a particular region to start farms and communities, the focal point of the church homecoming or anniversary is the group of founders of each specific church, the "fathers of the congregation," the progenitors of the "family of faith." In some of the homecoming worship services the pictures of founders are actually displayed during the service; in others, they are reproduced in the bulletin. Many small churches have produced a local history, a chronicle of the early founders and of the church's changes over the years; this may be for sale at the homecoming. In the Presbyterian congregations the church founders are also the earliest elders of the congregation, and the official minutes of the church session form a careful documentation of the history of each local church since its founding. This written tradition provides a link with the institutional church and with the regional denominational history; the people of the assembled homecoming group provide the social expression of the interlocking descent groups, all of whom together form the contemporary version of the "children of God" or the "family of faith."

The church homecoming is an event familiar to all the Protestant denominations in the South, but it is associated historically with rural Presbyterians, Methodists, and Baptists. Throughout the 250 years of their history, the scattered country churches have held various versions of an annual outdoor reunion of the members, drawing those who were born and reared in the congregation and who have moved away.

In the Presbyterian congregations of the 1700s these gatherings coincided with the holding of communion, served only periodically in those congregations lacking a full-time pastor. Once or twice a year, when an ordained minister was sent out by the Synod of Philadelphia, communion would be given. The occasion would be shared by several neighboring congregations.

Thompson points out that as the churches of the frontier became more a part of the established order of Presbyterianism and as the country became more densely settled, the camp meeting itself began to take the form more of a "protracted meeting." In these protracted meetings people returned to their homes at night, but the services would actually last for several days, he says, "in accordance with Scottish tradition. . . ." He refers to these times as "communion season" (Thompson 1963a:226).

In his history of Presbyterian worship in America, Julius Melton notes that the writing of the Presbyterian Directory of Worship in 1787 was fraught with disagreements between urban and rural committee members, with the rural members being ". . . fond of sacramental seasons, those series of services surrounding the sacrament which drew crowds of worshipers from the countryside" (Melton 1967:26). Those favoring even quarterly communion, and certainly anyone suggesting that communion be held on a weekly basis, were in danger of being identified with the formalized tradition of Episcopalian and Roman Catholic practice. The annual outdoor services provided an especially efficacious means of expressing one's theological purity. Within the activities of a homecoming or communion gathering the themes of the sacred place, the founding ancestors of the congregation, and the ancestors buried in the graveyard are all present. The past and the present are tied together in ways similar to those of the Scottish outdoor meetings.

A survey of the local histories of several early Presbyterian churches in Virginia, North Carolina, and South Carolina reveals that these congregations were each established between 1740 and 1789 by groups of families who had emigrated into Virginia from Pennsylvania and then moved on down from Virginia into the Carolina Piedmont. The Old Stone Church in Augusta County, Virginia, was the earliest of this network, receiving the first settled Presbyterian pastor south of Maryland in 1740. Founders of this and the network of early churches in the Shenandoah Valley and in the Carolinas were emigrants and children of emigrants from Ulster and from Scotland, moving usually in groups of kinspeople to establish farms in the backcountry of the colonies in the open-country neighborhoods that would be tied together into Presbyterian congregations. Families from this church in the Valley of Virginia moved into upcountry South Carolina in the 1760s; and in 1789 the Old Stone Church of Oconee County, South Carolina, was founded.

The church history for this congregation records the information that one of the church fathers, General Andrew Pickens (1739–1817), who grew up in Augusta County, Virginia, came to South Carolina "with other associated families" and settled at Long Cane in Abbeville County. The church history lists other founders as "several men from Abbeville, including General Pickens, Colonel Robert Anderson" and others, totaling forty families. The church founders and their families were buried in the graveyard adjoining the church. The local historian reports that the Oconee Stone Church and Cemetery Association was formed in 1893 "to preserve the old church and cemetery and to compile a history with the cooperation of two chapters of the D.A.R."[2] From church records and histories this period emerges as one in which many such associations were formed to protect old churches and cemeteries, to honor the founders and, in some cases, to celebrate centennials of church founding, as in this instance. In this late nineteenth-century period the farming economies of the South also were being disrupted by changes and populations were shifting away from the countryside into the mill towns and into the cities.

A second example of a church in the early Presbyterian congregations in the Virginia to Carolina network was the Sugar Creek Presbyterian Church in Mecklenberg County, North Carolina, which received its first pastor, shared jointly with the congregation of the Rocky River Presbyterian Church, in 1758. This first pastor was Alexander Craighead, who was born in Augusta County, Virginia, and who was well known for his teaching and preaching on the covenants of the early Scottish reformers, which he believed were still binding. Craighead's six daughters were married during his long pastorate at the Sugar Creek Church, forming the beginnings of an associated kin group. Craighead's son became a Presbyterian minister. His son was asked by the church to accept a call to the pastorate in later years but refused. Subsequently, his grandson, Samuel Craighead Caldwell, became pastor for thirty-five years, and later his great-grandson John Madison McKnutt Caldwell served as the church's pastor from 1837 to 1846.[3]

The Rocky River Presbyterian Church history was published in the same year as that of Sugar Creek, 1954, in anticipation of the anniversary of 200 years of these two congregations. In 1970 the church historian, Thomas Spence, told me that "at Rocky River they still have communion twice a year—the first Sunday in May (the May Meeting or sometimes called the homecoming) and the last Sunday in September or first in October." He attributed this partly to the tie-in with the Covenanters through Craighead. He suggested that the May time had been set earlier because it was "after the roads were passable" and that the October one was chosen because it is "before the cold weather sets in." In the outdoor meal that followed, he described a dinner on the grounds in which each family had a separate table—"I mean big families, sometimes twenty or thirty people, the whole group sat together. Then some young fellow decided it wasn't very democratic and changed to one table sometime around the 1930's."[4]

Another in the cluster of interconnected churches of this early period was Hopewell Presbyterian Church in North Carolina, whose founding families also came from Virginia and whose sons and daughters married the sons and daughters of the other Presbyterian congregations.[5] The graveyards of Sugar Creek, Steele Creek, Rocky River, Popular Tent, and Hopewell Presbyterian churches tell the story of these transgenerational ties. And those who left with their families in clusters of kin and friends in the early 1800s to settle west of the Appalachians or to venture down into North Alabama or North Florida have left their testimony of kin group connections in the graveyards of daughter churches. The Presbyterians buried their dead in churchyards, following the traditional Scottish pattern, while the predominant pattern of Baptists, Methodists, and other assorted Protestants on the western frontier was to bury their dead in open-country community cemeteries donated by one of the family heads; this resulted in a cemetery of related families buried together with no church or town nearby. Therefore, when the Presbyterian congregations gather to honor their ancestors, they are celebrating both the founding of their local congregation and the expression of a religious community coterminous with the actual social and economic community.

The Presbyterians spring from that tradition in Calvinism that emphasizes the covenant people and the community of the saints, teaching at the same time the doctrines of predestination and the body of the elect as the body of the church that is visible in this world. The connection between saints and ancestors is clear in the church homecoming or the church reunion, where founders are buried beside the church and descendants have dinner on the grounds close to the graveyard. The saints of the Protestant tradition, those who have been faithful followers of the church and its doctrines, are the elect, or the "people of God." These individuals tamed the wilderness and raised families, and they did this in response to a "calling" to be a faithful Christian and to witness their own salvation by living the good life. The church records attest to the good life lived by these ancestors and to their dedication to the cause of spreading the gospel through sending out their own sons and daughters into newly opened territories, where new Presbyterian congregations would be founded. It is a collective version of the American dream—a version of the imperative to move on and seeks one's fortune that is couched within the context of long-standing religious and cultural tradition, a tradition emphasizing communal life and expressed socially in tight-knit communities of cocongregationalists who will all enter into the Kingdom of Heaven together and whose heavenly life will be an extension of their godly life on earth.

Of the May meeting at the Rocky River Presbyterian Church, Thomas Spence, who served as pastor, gives the following account of the ceremonial statement of these meanings.

It is the day of days, as it were, the Christian Counterpart of the Passover, Pentecost, and Tabernacles all combined in one.

The May Meeting not only reflects the joy of the treasured feasts of Israel, but stands as an earnest of that uninterrupted gathering around the Father's Table, when the saints of all ages shall drink anew of the fruit of the vine in the blessed Kingdom of their Redeemer. It is not only a backward look . . . to the days of . . . Alexander Craighead, John Makemie Wilson and Daniel Lindley . . . but a prospect of the time when they, and those who follow them across the intervening years, shall assemble in the house not made with hands, at the end of the age, beside the waters of another River, which flow forever by the throne of God.   (Spence 1954:168–169)

Throughout the nineteenth century, when the movement westward was in its prime phase, the Presbyterians of North Carolina who remained behind continued to be affiliated in networks of congregations and of families. The Appalachian Mountains became the border between the older, staid, conservative, communally oriented Presbyterians and the newer, individualistic believers in the personalistic Calvinism of the frontier. Weisberger, in describing this rift regarding the question of revivalistic religion, gives the following account of the division from 1800 to 1810.

The Presbyterians were vulnerable, because there were, at this time two Presbyterian worlds. The Presbyterianism of New England and the Mid-Atlantic states was the child of seventeenth-century Puritanism. It was intellectually majestic, training its ministers, mainly at Princeton and Yale, to deliver sermons heavily weighted with learning in ancient and modern tongues. Its congregation were drawn from the successful classes of the countryside and supporting towns.

But as one moved southward and westward, one found Presbyterian flocks gathered mostly from Scotch-Irish who were taming the frontier.
                                                            (Weisberger 1958:38)

It was in this time period, beginning in 1809, that the early frontier revivals captured the imagination of these frontier Scotch-Irish and provided the format for the beginning of the third type of outdoor gathering that has become a pilgrimage to a sacred place—the camp meeting.

The Camp Meeting

The Clear Creek Camp Meeting in North Georgia is always held in the first week of August and has met annually since 1840, with a few years off for the War Between the States. Families use the campground for their reunions on successive Sundays in summer, opening the family "tent" or cabin at that tme. But the real event for which the campground exists is the camp meeting, which will draw 300 to 400 people for preaching services on the opening Sunday and keep 100 of them there for the week, visiting, eating, singing, and hearing two sermons every day. It is not affiliated with any denomination, although its families are regular members of Methodist, Baptist, or Presbyterian churches. The guest preacher is a Methodist this year, as he has been every year for the past ten years or so. A Methodist bishop regularly visits to preach on opening day. A professor at the Methodist theology school is a member of one of the oldest camp meeting families. And just down the road at the Pleasant Grove Camp Meeting most of the members are Baptist, and their guest preacher comes from a large Baptist church in a nearby town. And at Salem Camp Ground the speakers are usually Presbyterian. Clear Creek Camp Meeting begins with a worship service on a Sunday morning, but the worshippers have been arriving and moving into family tents since the day before.

At the service, good old-fashioned hymns are featured; a song leader stands before the group to lead the singing, and a piano accompanies the congregational renditions of the hymns selected from the Wesleyan Hymnal. The featured speaker of the week has been carefully chosen for his oratorical abilities. He will have a theme, and his series of evening sermons will follow that theme. Attenders who are unable to stay over for the week will drive out to the services in the evenings after work; the week-long attenders will hear a different speaker in the mornings, and the women and men will hold separate Bible studies and prayer groups in the afternoons. On this Sunday the sermon is well received and, after its conclusion, the preacher gives a traditional "altar call" in which those who wish to renew their commitment to Jesus Christ are invited to come forward and indicate their willingness to renounce sinful ways and live a faithful life. Those who respond have been forward many times before. On one or more evenings some individual will come forward who has never publicly professed his or her faith. Conference with the minister after the service will direct this person's interest to a local Methodist or other church so that the person can become a part of an ongoing congregation. A benediction ends the service, and the worshippers turn about to one another as visiting with friends becomes the primary activity.

The meal following the Sunday service is held outdoors in the open-air style so familiar for these meetings; for the rest of the week each meal will be prepared before services by the women who had taken up residence for the time of the camp meeting. On weekdays each large family will eat together inside their cabin at the long table that will seat fifteen to twenty family members. Clear Creek is a small campground of only twenty-four cabins, set in a semicircle around the open area and the arbor. Many of its families live in the towns and countryside nearby. Most work in the towns while keeping a small farm or a small plot of land for gardening. Billy Harper, who organizes and coordinates the food and activities at the Harper tent, is a practical nurse. Her daughter Faye is a doctor's receptionist and her son-in-law works for the telephone company as a lineman. Her brother Bobby is a carpenter, another brother is an electrician, and her husband works for the gas company. The farmers, homemakers, and workers mingle together at camp meeting with others from the area whom they have known all their lives. Their cousins from Atlanta or from various large towns further south will drive up for the Sunday services and then drive back home that evening.

Other camp meetings in the North Georgia area are larger and more elaborate, such as that at Salem Camp Ground near Covington, where in 1978 a rambling white frame Salem hotel offered "board for $2.50 per person per day" and picnic facilities are available for "special groups such as civic clubs, Sunday School Classes, Men's Clubs, and other special groups."[6] Classes are taught for each separate age group of children and adults by a staff of seven teachers; gold, blue, and red ribbons are given for perfect or near-perfect attendance at classes and preaching services. The daily schedule at Salem is a full one, including performances by church choirs from congregations as far away as Dothan, Alabama, and a choir known as the Coca-Cola Company Choir of Atlanta. The morning services every day are broadcast on the local radio station. An Atlanta journalist described the scene at Salem Camp Ground in the following story for the *Atlanta Constitution.*

> CONYERS—The present tabernacle at Salem Camp Ground was built in 1854 and smells of the freshly cut pine shavings that cover the dirt floor.
>
> The hand-hewn rafters are held together with the original pegs that Moses and Slider Presnel used before the Civil War to construct a meeting place for middle Georgia Methodists.
>
> While the stand is now equipped with fluorescent lights and a loud-speaker system, and people come in air conditioned cars rather than covered wagons, the preaching still inspires a faith that "endures from generation to generation."
>
> The 146th annual camp meeting began Friday and will continue through Aug. 16.
>
> At the service Sunday, over 1,000 people from across the state packed into the open tabernacle. . . .   (Murray 1974:6A)

Within the immediate vicinity of what is now the metropolitan area of Atlanta, Georgia, there are other old campgrounds of the type described for Clear Creek and Salem. Smyrna Campground near Smyrna was organized in 1833; Marietta Campground in 1837; Shingleroof Campground in Henry County in 1830; Smyrna Campground near Conyers in 1840.[7] The time of organization of these campgrounds coincides with the opening of the North Georgia area to its settlement by emigrants from the Carolina Piedmont and from East Tennessee in the wake of the removal of the Creek and Cherokee Indians in the early decades of the nineteenth century. The timing also coincides with the general trend of revivalistic religion on the frontier, in the early 1800s, which resulted in the rapid growth of the Methodist and Baptist denominations throughout the South and the new territories of the Midwest and Southwest. The old-style, staid, traditional Presbyterians of the Valley of Virginia and the Carolina Piedmont were not a part, to any large extent, of this camp meeting movement, although the Presbyterians of the western frontier were among its instigators and its followers. The split in the Presbyterian Church into several branches and then again splits from those branches into other sects and smaller denominational groups was related to the division over revivalistic religion in general, which had its primary social expression in the camp meeting.[8]

The first of the now-famous large outdoor revival meetings was held in Logan County, Kentucky, in 1800, followed shortly by the Cane Ridge meeting in Bourbon County, Kentucky, in 1801. At this meeting the organizer and preacher was Presbyterian minister Barton W. Stone, pastor of Concord and Cane Ridge Presbyterian churches in Bourbon County. Sweet (1964) describes the gathering as follows.

> Stone had made great preparations for the meeting, and a large area had been cleared, in the center of which a large tent had been erected, while the adjoining ground was laid off in regular streets along which the tents and lodges of the people were to be placed.   (Sweet 1964:87)

Estimates of attendance for this meeting went up to 10,000 to 20,000. Sweet reports that those for whom an actual record existed totaled 1100 communicants. These communicants were presumably the people who had to present themselves for approval and be issued communion tokens in order to take part in the communion service. Sweet reports a practice in the frontier Presbyterian churches that is reminiscent of Scotland. He says:

> A Communion sermon was first preached to be followed by what was called *fencing of the tables.* This was an exercise in which each member was examined and if any were found guilty of breaking any of the ten commandments they were debarred. Those who were qualified were given small lead disks, called *tokens,* which were collected by the elders after the communicants had seated themselves at the tables.
> (Sweet 1945:132)

Several variations of this practice are reported for the earliest outdoor meetings in Kentucky and Tennessee.

The themes of the camp meeting sermons seem at first glance to be at variance with the Calvinistic emphasis on communal life and covenant community. The camp meeting themes and those of revivalistic religion in general were what Sweet and others have called "personalized Calvinism." Personal salvation is emphasized, with the individual having the choice of responding to God. This emphasis on freedom of the will in some ways represents a break with the traditional Calvinistic emphasis on predestination and community. At the same time, it represents that aspect of Calvinistic belief that enables the person to become the lonely pilgrim walking on life's way, responsible for oneself as an individual instead of being bound in to the obligations of the small world of kinship and town life that was represented by Roman Catholic tradition. Weber (1905) points out that this type of individualization is essential for the spirit of risk associated with capitalism. The families who return to old camp meeting grounds for family reunions in the twentieth century and those who continue to attend camp meetings in the summer while being faithful capitalistic urban dwellers in the winter are embodying in their behavior an attempt to resolve the conflicts and contradictions inherent in these apparently unresolvable prescriptions of Protestant frontier faith and practice.

The tent meeting or tent revival as an event in the present day, as in the past in the Southern United States, is most often held by traveling preachers affiliated with sect groups and not with mainstream Protestant churches. As an outgrowth of the early camp meeting, it is aimed at evangelizing the unsaved, bringing religion to the unchurched, and herding the wild sheep of the frontier into flocks with a shepherd at their head. If this is properly accomplished by a traveling preacher, a group of the saved can be gathered into a continuing congregation, thus bringing the outdoor meeting indoors. The saved individuals eventually have historically enclosed their service themselves by building an edifice over the top of the meeting place and becoming institutionalized as a Methodist, Baptist, or other denominational church.

In his study of what he calls "plain-folk camp meeting religion 1800–1845," Dickenson Bruce has explained the camp meetings of the early nineteenth century as a religious response to the hard life of the frontier, an attempt to create an alternate world that is more pleasant than the one at hand. Of this alternate world he says:

> The plain-folk received "another world to live in" as a result of conversion. At one level, that other world was a heaven ʼwhere their troubles

would end forever; yet they also received "another world to live in" while they remained in this life. The saints described their new world in the language of evangelical Protestantism, but what they described was distinctly relevant to the place and time in which they lived.

(Bruce 1974:134)

He goes on to suggest that the conversion experience offered the individual a possibility of reconciling ideologically the gap between what "ought to be" and what "is," or the gap between secular and sacred worlds. Bruce seems to indicate that the converted individual then began to reconstruct his or her personhood in the image of the "saved" self and to live life within the total communal experience of the elect. He writes:

The convert's values were no longer founded on the hedonistic individualism of the frontier, but upon a desire to maintain the place in the community of the saints which each member had achieved by his conversion. Belief meant a complete redefinition of self in corporate rather than autonomous terms.   (Bruce 1974:134)

Protestant belief emphasizes both person and community. Neither the world of communal life nor the isolated individual exists in an either/or situation, but both the world of the individual and the world of the community are constantly competing for primacy within the total social framework of the Protestant individual. Both the churched and the unchurched experience the conflict of these two demands because the demands are deeply rooted in modern Western culture itself.

Bruce (1974) demonstrates that the early camp meetings are clearly a part of the tradition associated with the Southern "plain folk," those who were landholders of small tracts, who held no slaves, and who moved several times over a life career in order to get better land or to exploit opening territories. He characterizes this phenomenon in the following comments.

The Southern "frontier" was a condition rather than a particular geographical area. It was not simply that Southerners, like many other white Americans, were moving west, changing the continent into a land of farms, but rather that even the lands behind the line of European settlement in the South contained few established, stable communities. They remained sparsely populated regions, inhabited by people who

never stayed in one place for a very long period of time—a perpetual
frontier maintained by the continual quest for large numbers of white
Southern farmers for new land. . . .

New territories grew rapidly, from the opening of Kentucky in the
late eighteenth century to the colonization of the lower South and Texas
in the following century.   (Bruce 1974:14)

One can almost trace the dates of the establishment of camp meeting grounds in each Southern state by the dates of the opening of
that particular region for settlement by Europeans and Euro-Amer-
ican settlers. The earliest dates for campgrounds are in the early
years of the nineteenth century in Kentucky; we find North Georgia campgrounds with founding dates between 1825 and 1840, and
those in Texas were not found until the late nineteenth century.

In Texas, the western edge of the frontier during the late
nineteenth century, the camp meeting was an important form of
summertime gathering as it had been for parents of these same
settlers who came from Kentucky, Tennessee, or North Georgia.
The assembly provided a summer activity for farmers, ranchers,
and their town kinfolk. One of the best known of the meetings held
today in Texas is Bloys Cowboy Campmeeting near Fort Davis,
Texas, founded in 1890 by a Presbyterian minister sent as a frontier missionary from Illinois.[9] At the Bloys Campmeeting of the
1980s over 1000 people gather each August for the week of services, staying in their families' permanent cabins or in mobile
homes and recreational vehicles brought in for the occasion. Due to
the great distance of the meeting from any city or large town, there
are few commuters, and the assembly is populated for one busy
week by a collection of residents taking their annual vacation from
ranches and ranching towns. The families here are interrelated over
four or five generations, as are the families of the eastern camp
meetings in Georgia and Tennessee.

In the early camp meetings at Bloys, each family made a
"camp" with their wagons and brought a "chuck wagon." The
ranch chuck wagon cooks who cooked for cowboys on the range
came along. Now families assemble for meals in four large "cook
tents." Meals are prepared by cowboy cooks from several ranches.
Each large cooking and eating shed will serve several hundred
people three times a day. The people who eat together in each shed
and who are connected by ties of marriage and kinship are also

predominantly members of the same denomination—Methodist for one cluster, Presbyterian for another, Baptist for the third, and Disciples of Christ for the fourth. There is a great deal of visiting from camp to camp at mealtime, with in-laws moving from one camp to another and guests who come for the first time or who do not have a tie of kinship moving from camp to camp. No money is collected during the camp meeting, but a voluntary gift is given at the end by each family head to cover the costs of feeding that family during the week. Each family who has built one of the permanent cabins pays dues to the meeting association for the expenses of keeping up the grounds and paying the guest preachers and music directors.

The religious services are held twice a day in the massive arbor, known as the tabernacle; certain preachers are featured morning and evening alternately, and one preacher is included from each of the four denominations represented most heavily by the member families. Bible study is also a daily feature in the early morning and prayer meetings in the late afternoon. Children and young teens are led in special youth activities. In the evening, after the last benediction has been pronounced, families gather in the open air of the cool mountain nights to chat and sing under the stars and to share refreshments of pie, cake, coffee, and soft drinks and to sit up late enjoying the exchange of gossip, joking, and stories of the past.

Stories here are stories of life on the range and in the early ranching world. They are the stories of roundups, of fencing the open country, of cattle disputed and men killed or taken away to jail, of family feuds over land boundaries or cattle ownership, of neighboring with one another to get through a drought or a flood or to help each other past a crisis in the death of a husband or wife, the birth of a baby, the illness of a person who needed a doctor from miles away. The men spin their yarns at the men's prayer tree in the afternoons, and the women spin their tales of hardship and joy to one another sitting on the porches, watching the children or grandchildren. Families tell stories of their own mothers and grandmothers, of hard times on the ranches, and of the early days at the camp meeting. For most of the families at this camp meeting there is no other family reunion—all the reunion activities take place here, under the cook sheds at the prayer tree and in the arbor, on the porches, and under the stars. Family relationships are woven from summer to summer, and children are receivers of an ongoing tradition rooted in their own cultural heritage.

In each version of the camp meeting, meanings are created through the gathering of the families who identify with this place and with each other in a particular religious communal life. For the Georgia and Tennessee camp meeting, a sense of sacredness of place is created among people who live within a scattered but accessible area and who also are likely to attend family reunion in that same location. In Texas and on the frontier, camp meeting is a place to be revered in itself as the location for maintaining order and civility in a region being gradually claimed for towns and organized into discrete properties out of a previously untamed land.

There are no ancestors buried at campgrounds. The people who attended and attend these summer gatherings are permanently attached to local congregations and to local communities where their kin and ancestors are laid to rest; but the ancestors of the campground fall into the same category as the founders of the local church, and they are often remembered in sermons or in discussions as "the founders." Their descendants continue to attend the camp meeting and to carry on the old family names through the names of the cabins and cook sheds. However, like the cemetery gatherings and the church homecomings, the camp meetings are arranged and organized by "associations," those affiliated families who have joined together to collect annual contributions and/or dues for the upkeep of the sacred place and the veneration of the tradition. A prominent feature of many of the camp meetings is the Memorial Service, held on a Saturday afternoon to honor those who have died during the past year. For this service flowers are placed in memory of deceased members by their families and friends, and eulogies are spoken by various ministers in remembrance of the individuals who are gone. The names of all these are read out at the beginning and the end of the service, a custom that is also practiced at the devotional services of cemetery associations and of some family reunions.

At one camp meeting in North Georgia situated on the grounds of a country Presbyterian church, the afternoon service on Sunday is noted as the "homecoming service." This particular camp meeting advertised in 1974 that it has been "held annually for 147 years." In the homecoming service the preaching, hymns, and recognition of founders and their descendants resemble the order and content of the church homecomings of the same region. Longevity of life and of devotion to the camp meeting is recognized by the leader of the worship, who asks for a show of hands by those who have attended the camp meeting every year for eighty, then seventy, then sixty, and on down to ten years. One hardy soul responded in 1974 that she had attended faithfully for eighty years, four for seventy, nineteen for sixty years, five for fifty years, fifteen for forty years, and four, seven and five for thirty, twenty, and ten years each. This gives a total of sixty-nine participants who had attended every year for ten or more years.

The camp meeting stands beside the church homecoming and the cemetery reunion as an event symbolizing the ongoing life of a connected community of people in kin groups. These kin groups either *sent out* their daughters and sons, or were founded by those who *were sent*, or both, as in the case of the Piedmont Presbyterians. In all three settings we find pilgrims reassembled who have gone out from their homes on individual searches for achievement and success. In the case of many, they have gone out not alone as wanderers but as couples and as families looking for a new land to settle and tame, branching, splitting away from earlier couples and families who had tamed earlier lands. The individual life as a pilgrimage is one that is lived in tension between seeking one's fortune and preserving one's communal traditions. The annual religious assembly at the church, the graveyard, and the camp meeting grounds is one way of resolving the tensions within the cultural system—a system that has built into it contradictory prescriptions that are impossible to fulfill. Again, as in the family reunion, individuals are allowed to fulfill all demands, to be true and faithful Christians, to belong to an ongoing congregational community while still being free to pursue the successes of the American dream.

The meaning of "community" is generated within this framework. The notion of community, which has been battered about so often by sociologists and anthropologists from Toennies to the present may, in fact, be an idea that is in itself a product of these contradictory demands. If "blood, soil, and mind" are truly the ingredients of European local residential community, then these ingredients are also present in the assembled temporary communi-

ties of reunion, homecoming, and camp meeting. And it is possible
that the disruption to economy and society at the time of the
Reformation were accompanied by other shifts in worldview to
make any approximation of Toennies' local community impossible. The pilgrimage of the Protestant, then, is not one that leads *out
there* to seek the saint's shrine and to work out his or her salvation.
It is one that leads *back to* a network and an ideal—a community of
faith and of location that is ingrained within Protestant ideology,
one in which the family of faith, the people of God who have been
already saved by Grace, can fulfill His demands and also can "be
fruitful and multiply and subdue the earth. . . ."

   The sacred place is seen here as church, cemetery, and camp
meeting ground. In the first the sacred place is enshrined through
gathering in honor of the founders of the congregation, who are
also buried in the churchyard if one exists side by side with the
church. In the second, the rural cemetery not connected to the
church is sacralized through recurrent gathering to honor the dead
and to reaffirm membership in the connected kin groups descended
from the honored ancestors. In the third, the camp meeting ground
becomes sacred as an expression of the outdoor church, that symbolic statement of antiestablishment and nonhierarchical tradition
that also includes founders of the faith and interlocking kin groups.
In the denominational summer conference center and cottage community one sees the most elaborate version of sacred place and of
enshrined kinship; this sacred community is described and inter-
preted in Chapter Five.

CHAPTER FIVE

Covenant Community— The Denominational Conference Center

THOSE WHO ATTEND family reunions, church and cemetery home-comings, and camp meetings in the summer fall into an overall pattern of gathering and dispersal that defines the Protestant community and the Protestant individual. By going one's separate way and yet returning periodically to affirm one's affiliation with a broader network of kin, friends, and congregation, the Protestant pilgrim fulfills his or her calling to be faithful. The symbolic center for the gathering of the faithful within each denomination is the denominational summer community or conference center, where all the themes of sacredness can come into play. One such pilgrim center is the community I have studied in depth, the conference center and cottage community of Presbyterians at Montreat, North Carolina.[1]

Montreat

Montreat, North Carolina, is the central pilgrim shrine for Southern Presbyterians. The name, a shortened form of mountain retreat, is an appropriate label for the small community tucked away in the mountains with its strong stone buildings lining the valley, flanked by family cottages along the ridges on each side. All the trappings of a true shrine are present there. One enters through a tall stone archway known as "the gate," an edifice that separates Montreat from the secular world. It is the only entrance to the bounded community, guarding access to the one main road. Until recent years the gate was attended by a young man who checked each entrant's gate pass, purchased through the conference center. Only appropriate entrants were allowed in by the "gate boy," the classic boundary-keeper, preserving the selectivity and seclusion of the retreat center. Although there is no longer a gate boy, the gate itself remains as a symbol of entry into a sacred world.

The new arrival at Montreat travels past the gate down Assembly Drive, named for the Presbyterian General Assembly, past streets and roads bearing the name of each of the synods in the territory of the southern denomination—Texas Road, West Virginia Terrace, North Carolina Terrace, and the other Southern states. At the center of the grounds is a cluster of hotels and dormitories where conference participants are housed during the summer season and that, in the winter, houses a small church college. In the heart of the conference center stands the auditorium, which seats more than 1000 people for Sunday morning worship and for the daily preaching services of the conferences.

In a Protestant pilgrim shrine in the Presbyterian tradition, one would expect to find material expressions of a culture that values communality, evangelism, and an educated laity. Near the auditorium are these expressions: the community center, the World Missions Building, and the bookstore. The pilgrims come for the healing power of the surrounding natural beauty, for the regenerative elixir of fellowship, for the renewal of great singing and preaching services, and for the enhanced understanding that comes from reading and studying the Bible, studying church history and doctrine, and listening to teachers and worship leaders who espouse the virtues of the informed, ordered, intelligent life. Montreat is a mixture of a Chautauqua and a frontier camp meeting, overlaid on a base of family and kinship loyalty and annual regathering.

The family and kinship aspects of Montreat do not become immediately visible to the first-time attender of conferences, whose purpose is to gain information and inspiration through worship and study. The activities centered on kinship can be entirely separate from the conference season activity, overlapping only because some of the conference teachers and preachers belong to the large family groups and some of the vacationing families have members who drop in on the conference services. It is common for individuals to come to their family cottage for vacations at Montreat over a period of years without taking part in any of the conferences. The family cottages are scattered along the high ridges or nestled along the creek so that they are almost hidden from view by the dense mountain foliage. An entire extended kin group may vacation in one of these cottages during the summer, with clusters of siblings visiting together at the cottage of their parents, bringing along all the spouses and children for a merry overflow. The cottages are really quite large houses, many of which have been handed down through one family for several generations. Several Montreat families have built a series of houses along one road, creating lines and clusters of kin-related cottagers—brothers, sisters, and cousins—who entertain their children and grandchildren here in the summer. The total effect is that of a kaleidoscope of family reunions concurrently forming and disbanding in an ebb and flow that matches weekends and summer holidays. Montreat becomes one big kin-religious homecoming, with the old people reminiscing about days gone by when they were children playing in the creek and climbing Lookout Mountain, the middle generations discussing denominational politics and family news, and the young people playing in the creek or climbing Lookout. At mealtime four generations may sit together and tell stories over the fresh vegetables bought from a local vendor; after meals there is a transgenerational cleanup. The place is a swarm of activity. It is a shrine to extended kinship and to transgenerational community, enacted in human activity in all its most sacred forms.

The rhythms of activity at Montreat are established partly because Montreat is the official conference center for the Presbyterians of the Southern United States. Every summer several thousand people gather here to attend various conferences organized for the continuation of education among lay Christians and for their religious renewal in a setting removed from the ordinary distractions of everyday life. In late May the community of Montreat is almost completely deserted, with the small college that shares the buildings and grounds with the conference center having disbanded for the year and the summer conferences not having begun. In late

May the year-round residents gradually start to brush up the roads and buildings for the annual onslaught of summer people; as the rhododendrons and mountain laurels begin to bloom, the summer people arrive.

By the first of June families are moving into summer cottages. The mothers of small children come to stay for the entire summer, with the fathers commuting from Charlotte, Gastonia, or Atlanta on weekends and for vacation. Retired people move in for the summer to host the succession of children, grandchildren, and other relatives who will come and go for the next three months. Professors at church colleges and seminaries move into cottages where they will work on books and papers while their families visit and play. By the middle of June the troupe of summer workers have arrived who will run the swimming pool, serve the tables in the Assembly Inn, clean the dormitory rooms, repair the roads, collect the garbage, move the chairs at the auditorium, show the films, call the square dances, and serve as counselors at the children's day camp. "The Collegiates," as the workers are called, are members of a work force composed of approved Presbyterian young people who are students at the denominational colleges or who may be students at a secular university if they are members of established Presbyterian families. Many are children of parents who worked at Montreat in their own youth. By late June the first conference will begin.

The conferences at Montreat are organized by church boards and agencies in Atlanta and are coordinated by the permanent staff of the Mountain Retreat Association and the Montreat Conference Center. The conferences attract attenders who are elders in congregations, officers in the Women of the Church, members of local Christian Education Committees and Music Committees, and interested laypeople who wish to participate in workshops and listen to speakers on Christian families, youth work, the Bible, world missions, or on specific topics of current interest that rotate through the conference schedule each summer. Conferences assemble in the large auditorium at the center of the Montreat cove. The auditorium is constructed of steel girders arching over a circular enclosure, resembling the architecture of a camp meeting arbor, except that it is completely enclosed and is heated and air conditioned.

Classroom buildings nearby, which serve as college classrooms in the winter, become the location for group discussions and workshops during conferences. The Presbyterian Historical Foundation building holds the collection of all the church session minutes, beginning with the earliest Presbyterian congregation in the South, and provides archives and resources for research. A Presbyterian bookstore is housed in a central building, where Sunday School literature is available along with works in theology, church history, religious education, and other topics of interest to the educated layperson.

Conference attenders stay in dormitories or in the old hotel, the Assembly Inn; they have their meals together either in the dormitory cafeteria or in the hotel, family style at large tables. Some people who have moved into the cottages for their summer-long residence also attend one or more conferences or drop in on the conference speakers in the auditorium. Both groups are attending Montreat for the mixed purposes of receiving spiritual renewal through listening to sermons and attending workshops and receiving social refreshment through the enjoyment of "fellowship" with other like-minded individuals whose ongoing participation and commitment to the denomination match their own. An additional goal is sought by those who live in the cottages summer after summer—the goal of renewing ties of kinship with extended families who reassemble each summer in the cool mountains and within the comfortable fold of friendship and shared community that Montreat offers.

The assembly buildings at Montreat are constructed of grey native stone, built primarily by local craftsmen in the early years of the century. Their starkness and imposing nature remind the observer of forbidding castles in North Britain or of the stone forts of early America. The summer cottages are mostly wood frame dwellings on the order of large rural farmhouses, sturdy and sedate, with long porches wrapping around them. Many are perched atop steep inclines approached by flights of steps. The reward for climbing to the porch is the panoramic view of the mountains beyond the cove. Other cottages line the road that skirts the creek, gaining as a compensation for the lost view the background noise of water rushing down the mountain. Many cottages have been completely modernized to provide some comforts for summer living. Others remain essentially old-fashioned rural houses with only the basic amenities of electricity and indoor plumbing but without insulated walls, modern kitchen equipment, or updated decor. In an attempt to get "close to nature" and "back to basics," those who stay in cottages like to see themselves as "camping" or "roughing it" and prefer to do without some of the city's conveniences such as television and microwave ovens. Those who stay in the conference dormitories give up the luxury of the Holiday Inn style of accommodation to share baths, sleep in dormitory beds, and eat cafeteria food as part of their own outdoor retreat experience. While the houses are more opulent than the "tents" and cabins of a camp meeting and the dormitories are more comfortable than the trailers and recreational vehicles brought to the campground parking lot, the participants are all involved in the same process of negating their city and town comforts for a rural experience that is comparatively austere.

In the rhythms of summertime life at Montreat there is a comfortable alternation between high peaks of conference activity and low points when the cottagers have the cove all to themselves for a day or two between conferences. The peak activity involving the entire community comes on the Fourth of July, when each of the children's "clubs"—the label used to denote the various age groups in the day-camp program—fashions a float for the parade, representing an aspect of Montreat life. In the Fourth of July celebration there are contests among children—greased pole climbing, watermelon eating, sack races—and tennis and swimming for everyone, followed by a cottage owners' picnic, a community square dance, and fireworks.

The conference season is over by the middle of August, the collegiate workers pack up and go back home before college starts again, and the cottage owners close up their houses for another season and return gradually to their life in the town and the city. The summer community has created itself once again in that expanse of sacred time between Memorial Day and Labor Day that Americans code as "summer," and it has again disbanded to disperse its participants into their roles within the secular, structured system.

The Creation of the Sacred Community

Montreat was first envisioned in the 1890s by a group of ministers, industrialists, and land developers in the Northeastern United States as a combination mountain resort and Christian retreat center. It was to resemble the Chautauqua community of New York and the similar gathering spots for religious and intellectual study at Northfield, Massachusetts, and Ocean Grove, New Jersey. One early pamphlet by John R. Collins of New Haven, Connecticut, features a map of the routes of the Southern Railroad and mentions a lecture and publicity by the Southern Railroad promoting the North Carolina mountains, complete with a slash in fare to one-half price for anyone attending the 1898 assembly at "Mountain Retreat."[2] In the same year a promotional booklet advertises the opening of "a mountain health resort and Christian community with temporary and permanent residence, similar in general plan to Ocean Grove, N.J., but under the management of Christians of every name instead of those of one denomination." In only a few years, Montreat was to become affiliated with one denomination, the Presbyterians, as Ocean Grove is affiliated with the Methodists. The pamphlet continues that the management of this new community would be "safe and conservative," and that it would provide residence "not only for Christian people but for those of good habits as well." There were to be "no saloons" and "The temptations, allurements to evil, bewilderments, and unsettling conditions of the modern city would be reduced to a minimum."

The location of Mr. Collins' ideal Christian community was found, with the assistance of those of the investors who were connected with the Southern Railroad,[3] "on the railroad about fifteen miles east of Asheville . . . the entrance being about one and a half miles north of Black Mountain Station." At that time Asheville was already considered "a famous health resort" and had enjoyed the benefit of being "about twenty-two hours by rail from New York, and can be reached from that city without a change of cars."[4] Mr. Collins, who served as the president, promoter, and organizer was apparently concerned from the beginning about the connection between the creation of the ideal Christian community and the motivation of making a profit on the devout travelers and

potential property owners. In 1921, he wrote of his early fears in a
letter to an associate. Of the 1898 time period, he says:

> Mr. Huyler, of New York, a year or two later built the first hotel, and
> paid up all the indebtedness. Mr. Huyler was very, very sincere in all he
> did, but as a fact, I think some of the men next to him thought they had a
> big chance to make a lot of money through the development of the place
> later. . . . I told him . . . if he ever diverted it for other purposes it
> would be a sacrilege and he would regret it to the end of his days.[5]
>
> (Collins 1921:1)

Several early summer assemblies held at Montreat are described in letters and diaries as if they resembled very much the
frontier camp meetings but with the added aspiration of becoming
something more—aspirations modeled on the assemblies of the
well-established New York and New England Chautauqua meetings and continued in the educational programming of the present
day. By 1907 the investors in the Northeast had turned their
attentions elsewhere, and the Mountain Retreat that had begun
with high hopes as an ideal Christian community was redefined.
The General Assembly of the Presbyterian Church in the United
States bought the assembly grounds from its previous owners and
retained the name of Mountain Retreat, shortening it to Montreat.
In fact, the "Mountain Retreat Association" was at its inception a
stock company in private hands with no formal connection to the
denomination but, as one historian of Montreat admits, "most of
whom were Presbyterians" (Anderson 1948). Later these owners
deeded their stock to the church to be held in trust. It was a minister
from Charlotte, North Carolina, in the heart of the Presbyterian
population and in the heart of the New South industrial textile
region who first interested the denomination in Montreat as a
conference center, and Montreat's first president of this new era
was from Gastonia, another heavily industrialized mill town. Anderson tells us in his history that between 1920 and 1925, in a
period of prosperity for the industrializing United States, a number
of large contributions were made to the grounds by various individuals who had made their fortunes in cotton textiles, mercantile
companies, building and engineering firms, and other growing
commercial enterprises of the Carolina Piedmont.[6]
During this same period in the early years of the century after

the Presbyterians had taken hold of Montreat, the first permanent cottages were built. Lots were sold for $100 each to those who wished to take part in this new summer center, and the industrialists of the Carolina Piedmont quickly constructed summer lodgings to take their families away from the heat and diseases of the rapidly degenerating atmosphere of the industrial towns into the cool haven of the mountains to be among other suitable families. The community began to become an elite summer community, similar to its models in the Northeast, where the wealthy owners of factories and industries of industrial cities could withdraw with their children into pleasant resorts for the summer while the people remaining in cities were left to work and to swelter in the summer heat.

In the Presbyterian summer community the organizers and administrators continued to conceptualize their mission as one of providing a spiritual home, while recognizing at the same time the value of keeping together those interconnected families in the "household of faith" who would form the core of the ongoing generations of the community of believers. In describing this double aspect of Montreat one of its primary supporters and early presidents, Dr. Anderson, writes of the "Montreat Spirit" in his history of Montreat, which resembles the local histories written of each Presbyterian congregation. He describes it as follows.

> The people of Montreat are the best people of our Church. They come from every section of the Church and perhaps as a class represent the cream of the Churches.

> . . . Separation from bad influences, the provision of the best spiritual food and spiritual environment, and association with one another are factors to aid our best people to live in the best way.
> (Anderson 1948:199)

Dr. Anderson's description of the overarching purpose and reason for being behind the community of Montreat is not unlike the description written by Dr. Spence of the May meeting of the Rocky River Presbyterian Church quoted earlier, describing the church homecoming. Both have captured the essence of the connections between the spiritual-ideological nature of the gatherings, reflecting Calvinistic theology and the idea of the covenant people, and the social-cultural nature of the same events, reflecting their power to mobilize large groups of people in ways that reinforce their own sense of belonging, commitment, and dedication. Anderson says:

> Montreat might be the revival of a long neglected Scriptural method to make strong and more effective the Kingdom of God upon earth. From the day of Moses to the day of Pentecost, embracing the entire Bible period from Moses to the Ascension of our Lord, under Divine direction and appointment, God's chosen people were called together three times a year in one place. These meetings were the Passover, Pentecost, and the Feast of Tabernacles. These three annual assemblies for worship ran parallel with the Presbyterian form of government from the day of Moses until the end of the New Testament age. These assemblies . . . were of unspeakable value during the Old Testament period to unify, co-ordinate, instruct, and inspire God's chosen people.
>
> Under the Divine order of things they were supplementary to the Presbyterian form of government and played just as important a part in promoting the interest of the Kingdom as did the form of government. . . .
>
> We Presbyterians have emphasized in our thought and doctrine the form of government, why have we so long minimized the practical value of its Biblical supplement, the three great annual popular meetings referred to above?
>
> . . . Moses, Elijah, John the Baptist and our Lord made use of large assemblies in the mountains as one of the most effective means to instruct, revive, and stimulate God's people to their noblest actions.
>
> (Anderson 1948:26-27)

Descriptions of early Montreat invariably refer to the goal of providing an ideal gathering of Christians in a community where preaching and instruction could take place. This goal fits with the creation of other such communities in the same time period by the Methodists at Ocean Grove, New Jersey, and later at Lake Junaluska, North Carolina. It also fits other Protestant gatherings responding to the same themes that had drawn their parents and grandparents into the revival camp meetings a generation or two before. In his history of revivalism in America, Weisberger (1958) points to the creation of the conference center at Northfield, Massachusetts, by Dwight L. Moody, famous revival preacher of the turn of the century, as an attempt to create a "religious Chautauqua, a "spiritual spa," where the best-known evangelical preachers of the time could be heard.[7]

The original summer educational-religious institution of this type at Chautauqua, New York, was started in an old camp meeting grounds in 1874 and gradually expanded to provide the role model for the others. In its heyday between 1924 and 1932, Sweet (1945) estimates that at Chautauqua "forty-five thousand people attended the general assembly each year where they heard famous preachers and lecturers, attended concerts, and in other ways absorbed culture." He says that "by the end of the century little Chautauquas had sprung up all over the country and many of them were utilizing old camp meeting grounds." Of those that were not utilizing old camp meeting grounds, most were constructing intentional summer communities that could serve these same purposes in a more organized and institutionalized way. These summer communities were closely linked with the formal denominational organizations and with the lives of the now successful and established merchants, owners of commercial enterprises, mills, and factories of the emerging industrial America, in this case of the New South.

The gradual formation of permanent summer assembly grounds for the Presbyterians in the South and in Texas is documented by E. T. Thompson in his comprehensive two-volume *Presbyterians in the South* (1963b) as one aspect of the growing interest in the early twentieth century in Christian education. While Montreat was developing as an institutionalized summer conference center, so was the conference center at Massanetta Springs, Virginia, fostered by the synod of Virginia, and also the center at Kerrville, Texas. At Kerrville a presbytery committee in 1906 organized summer gatherings for Presbyterians at a riverside in the hill country and called it "the Westminster Encampment." By 1914 it had become "a synod enterprise," and by 1932 it had developed into a full-fledged, permanent center with "a dining hall and an auditorium . . . a two-story roominghouse and forty cottages available for rent; forty-eight other cottages, privately owned, had been built on property belonging to the encampment" (Thompson 1963b:153). The development of this establishment and the one in Virginia closely parallels the growth and development of Montreat in North Carolina, and all three reflect an interest at the century's turn and through the 1920s with this type of separate summer center for what Thompson calls "the equipping of the saints." In his comments on the beginnings of Montreat, Thompson notes the conscious modeling after the religious summer communities of the Northeast by the founders of Montreat. He quotes a letter from one of the founders, J. R. Howerton, minister of the Charlotte First Presbyterian Church, in which Dr. Howerton wants to make Montreat "something of a Chautauqua, something of a Lake Winona, something of a Northfield, something more than any of these."[8]

The themes of camp meeting, Chautauqua, and utopian community come together in a number of summer denominational communities founded in the late nineteenth century by Presbyterian and Methodist idealists. In their earlier years most of these communities were owned outright by church organizations or by religious "associations" and governed in the manner of Calvin's Geneva, theocratic "cities of God." One noteworthy example is Ocean Grove, New Jersey, which was owned by a church Camp Meeting Association and governed in this theocratic fashion until 1980. (Montreat became a town under North Carolina laws in 1970; others have become secular entities in other years.) Ocean Grove was described in a magazine article in 1980 as "The town that made time stand still," and its anachronistic Sunday laws were described as follows.

> This community of 7000 year-round population, only 60 miles south of New York, has since 1869—the year of its founding by Methodists—been governed by a church Camp Meeting Association which laid down a strict set of Sunday blue laws: No swimming on the Sabbath; no cars on the streets from midnight Saturday to midnight Sunday; no hanging out of clothes on Sunday. It's been a throwback to the 17th century New England towns where the church reigned supreme.
>
> (Ryan 1980:4)

In anthropological terms these communities are the opposite of what this journalist calls "throwbacks." They are, instead, futuristic creations, inventions of shared vision of what life in towns "ought to be" according to Puritan faith and practice. Instead of making time stand still, they are creating sacred time and providing entry for modern people to experience an intentional communitas.

In the creation of the "little Chautauquas" and their elaboration into permanent summer facilities by each denomination, each denominational belief system and its theological underpinnings were, of course, called on to frame and give meaning to the enterprise. The Methodists would certainly be expected in this symbolic construction to call on the images associated with the old-time religion, with its "fellowship," its emphasis on love, brotherhood, the personal response of the individual to God through Jesus, and the teachings of Wesley and of the followers of this great preacher-teacher; Wesley and Wesleyan were popular names for regional camps and conference centers. The Methodist emphasis was more on individualistic education and less on the honor of founding ancestors and kin groups. The Presbyterians called on their own traditional symbolic inventory to give ideological shape to their summer communities, emphasizing Reformed themes and ancestors and naming their camps Westminster or John Knox. The meaning of Montreat and its smaller regional versions was, for the Presbyterians, not surprisingly, the assembly grounds for "the people of God," the "covenant people," the "covenant community," the "family of faith." This imagery runs through the definition of early Presbyterian Montreat and is predominant today in the verbal explanations given during Sunday sermons and conference introductions.

In the specific case of Montreat as the social expression of the ideological image of the covenant community, the people of God happened also to be the same people who were the captains of industry and the leaders of business enterprise across the Carolina Piedmont. Their attempt to form and to perpetuate their inner circle of families, who were predominantly Presbyterian in the rich textile region surrounding Charlotte and Gastonia, was aided considerably by the creation of a pleasant summer environment for their young to meet and fall in love. One imagines the youth of the early 1800s in this same region finding prospective mates in the joint congregational gatherings among the early churches at Rocky River, Sugar Creek, Poplar Tent, and all the rest, and in subsequent years in gatherings for church reunions and homecomings. Along with the emphasis on genealogy that arose in the United States during the 1890s with the creation of the First Families of Virginia, the Daughters of the American Revolution, the United Daughters of the Confederacy, the Daughters of the Republic of Texas, and other similar regional societies came the earliest social registers in various cities and the formation of college fraternities and, with coeducation, sororities. All these associations and clubs were focused primarily on the social purpose of creating an elite network of families in an otherwise class-free new nation that was growing helter-skelter without the safe traditions of older British and European antecedent countries.[9] Denominational summer communities were a part of this same thrust by the new industrial class of owners and managers, who were also stalwart Protestants, a group still known at Montreat as "devout industrialists."

In his study of the social and economic contexts of British and European traditions growing out of the late nineteenth century, Hobsbawm points out the social function of these traditions in the formation of elites in the new industrial society from 1870 to 1900. In Europe and in Britain, he says, the institutions of the aristocratic ruling class of the past provided the model for the new emerging "upper middle class." In the United States the creation of the tradition-centered associations focused on ancestry and on social position was "to establish an exclusive upper stratum among the white middle class" (Hobsbawm 1983:294). In addition to the various exclusive clubs and associations, he mentions the role of private schools in this process. He notes that private schools in both America and Britain were a means of establishing:

> social comparability between individuals or families lacking initial personal relations and, on a nation-wide scale, a means of establishing common patterns of behavior and values but also a set of interlinked networks between the products of comparable institutions and, indirectly, through the institutionalization of the "old boy," "alumnus," or "Alte Herren," a strong web of intergenerational stability and continuity.   (Hobsbawm 1983:293)

This same strong sense of alumni solidarity could be and was created among those who regathered for the summer conferences and for summer cottage vacations at the denominational community. Furthermore, this sense of interlinkage was and is forged even stronger by the fact that many of the participants also attend Presbyterian colleges, so that their relation to one another as alumni of Montreat is already in place when they become college friends, a friendship network extended when they work at Montreat in the summer as collegiate workers with other Montreat alumni who are attending other Presbyterian colleges. The resulting transgenerational elite network of families throughout the South is extensive in its reaches.

The attempt on the part of late nineteenth-century Presbyterians and other economically successful Protestants to create an ideal "community" rooted in Christian behavior and belief is a process bearing further examination. The same Presbyterians who founded Montreat are the descendants of persons who either left on their own initiative or were driven from Scotland and Ulster by the forces of rack-renting and other economic pressures to seek their fortunes in the New World. Their theology compelled them to assign causality to the Providence of God and to view themselves as a people moving under Divine authority into a new wilderness to establish a new life for themselves. In discussing this migration of the Scots in the middle 1700s into the Carolinas, Dickson declares that "To the emigrants the wilderness became an ocean and Moses an Ulster Scot" (Dickson 1966:12). As we have seen in the close scrutiny of the family reunion, those who moved again in subsequent generations into Tennessee and Texas were also following the individualized version of the command to subdue the earth and to give evidence of their salvation through their good lives. We find here again a set of contradictory prescriptions within the culture—the prescription to be the people of God as a communal entity, caring for one another, conflicting drastically with the prescription to respond to God's "calling" as an individual and to fulfill the expectation of hard work and the disciplined life.

Originally the covenant community was embodied in the clusters of related families who moved together and who lie now buried in the country churchyards and the open-country cemeteries. By the late 1800s the requirements of industrial society, the urbanizing textile regions, and the growing commercial centers and railroad towns were all taking their toll on the localized kinship-based congregational community. Those who wished to be a part of the rapidly changing new society and receive its rewards must indeed be ready to move again, this time to the new frontier of the town and city, and those who were successful faced the challenge of forming an industrial elite.

The Presbyterians of the Carolinas and adjacent states approached these new frontiers with some understandable ambivalence. Their steady stream into the comfortable refuge of the summer community of Montreat is one expression of the deep cleavage of values between the world of the city and the city of God. Montreat's early founders saw the city as wickedness and evil, the world of the Devil, and the denominational summer conference center as an alternate world, where the covenant community could be recreated.

Malcolm Chapman has studied the phenomenon of longing for security and stability among Highland Scots who have emigrated. The Scots, he says, have romanticized the vision of Celtic culture with their Clan and Gaelic language societies around the world. He attributes the romanticization of the Highlander partially to the process of the immigration itself. In this process, people who once saw their exit as a means to freedom and opportunity, to upward social mobility, once having attained these goals, now look back and seize on symbols of the past as a source of continuity in an otherwise discontinuous and ever-changing universe. This process is probably at work in the romantic imagery attached to all of the past communities of immigrants, resulting in a wealth of song and story. At Montreat we find it expressed in the impulse to create the ideal community that founders and participants envision might have existed at some past time in rural America.

Chapman points out that in nineteenth-century social theory there existed a similar fascination with the notion of "community," an interest that reached into the twentieth century with the invention of the conceptual dichotomy between rural and urban society and the study of urban sociology. He refers to this in the following passage.

> We have seen that the "community" became in the nineteenth century a locus for a variety of socially desirable characteristics. We have also seen that there were those who saw its disappearance as a potential emancipation from limiting and stunting restrictions. Folklore studies have on the whole adopted the former view, and many Gaels who choose to live in Glasgow have apparently accepted the latter before leaving, and the former upon having left.   (Chapman 1978:201)

There is clearly an ideological aspect to this discussion. In the case of the Protestant pilgrimages there is an ideal "good" attached to the small-scale, close-knit kin group and neighborhood while, at the same time, there is an ideal "good" attached to the individual person on a personal journey, a life-style that forces the individual away from that tight community way of life. Chapman notes that this dichotomy of ideals is also present in the theory and writings of sociologists, who have largely cooperated with the Protestants in creating this notion and transmitting it to generations of university students in its secular version.

> The essentially fictional nature of the idea of "community" in this context is expressed by Plant, who says that (his emphasis) "the notion of community is . . . implicitly defined in a conservative way in terms of a way of life which has been *lost*." (Plant 1974:28, quoted in Chapman 1978:201)

Argument about it is therefore not a simple regret for the passing of a well-observed phenomenon but, instead, "a debate fundamentally about the kind of society in which we *ought* to live" (Plant 1974:28, quoted in Chapman 1978:201).

Montreat as a community forms a commentary on the elaborate stratification of urban industrial society. It is egalitarian, communal, and simple in its style of life and patterns of consumption. And yet, the community itself is formed from the upper strata of Southern elite society; its inhabitants are the owners of the industries and the professional people who maintain medicine, law, academia, and the church. They are those who have the ability to own and keep up a summer cottage, either singly or in family clusters. They value education, and many have attended private colleges and universities; they value tradition, and many count their ancestors among the early distinguished Presbyterian settlers of the Carolinas. The community offers an opportunity for the simple virtues to be affirmed once again among a group of people whose daily lives are filled with complex layers of social differentiation. Within the fellowship of sameness—which the Montreat goers can sometimes be overheard referring to with the phrase "our kind of people"— those who are at the top of the social hierarchy of their individual towns and cities and at the top of the prestige scale in Presbyterianism can experience a society that purports to be nonhierarchical and completely unstratified. Montreat has, however, a fragile internal

stratification system of its own. Within the community of sameness
there exists difference based on one's membership in a kin group or
one's number of years of coming to Montreat.

The Kin Groups and the Household of Faith

In the years since 1909, when the Presbyterians assumed ownership of Montreat, over 400 cottages have been built along the roads
in the mountain valley and along the ridges. Each of these cottages
is owned by a separate family, a couple whose children all come in
the summers or a group of brothers and sisters who take turns using
it, with one or more weeks overlapping so that all the families can
visit together. One of the most pronounced features of social life in
Montreat is, in fact, the degree to which daily life is related to
kinship. A person is cataloged by other people primarily on the
basis not of profession or of the person's hometown or college, but
on the basis of the family to which the person belongs. This is
expressed in conversation as "Which Davis are you?" or "Now
who was your father?" and is followed invariably with an anecdote
about that person's relative whom the conversant knows. Leisure
activities center on kin group, too, with the children playing with
their cousins in the creek and going together to the daytime clubs
while their mothers, who are sisters and sisters-in-law, visit on the
porches, take trips together to nearby towns for supplies, and
provide care and entertainment for the older relatives. The elderly
aunts and uncles and grandparents, meanwhile, engage in their own
world of visiting and side trips with their own sisters, brothers, and
peers. The structure of kinship at Montreat is based on cognatic
descent, repeating the structure of kinship seen in the family reunion. In the Montreat community we find an elaborate set of
overlapping cognatic descent groups that are tied together by generations of intermarriage, resulting in a covenant community held
close by familial as well as religious bonds.

    The Montreat cottage is a symbolic house for the family and
kin group. It does not stand for the same status and prestige system
as the house of a nuclear family in the city, where the same family
might live in a modern dwelling in an upper-middle-class suburb
and where membership in a country club may further enhance

one's social position. Its rough exterior and spartan facilities stand for the high value on a simple life and on the closeness to nature of rural living. The Montreat cottage symbolism involves membership in a family of status within a sacred community whose members take their position from their links to the Presbyterian past and to the old churches of the ancestors. The cottage must be large enough to accommodate all the relatives who plan to visit during the summer. The porch is an important feature, for it is on the porch where the kin visiting takes place and where elderly women and men receive their young relatives who call and spend long hours chatting with old friends from their own Montreat youth. Inside the house, objects of sentimental importance dominate the furnishings and wall decoration. The "dining room table and chairs from Grandmother's house," old quilts and blankets, iron beds from farmhouses, the original house fittings from earlier days, and pictures of family members and of early Montreat all remind the member or the visitor that this family has a history and that these people "belong." Often the Montreat house is built near that of other relatives, with as many as four or five houses in a row belonging to a large kin group. A count of houses owned by people who were interrelated in 1970 revealed one network of relatives in which thirty-five houses were owned by the various families in one group.

The family reunion of most of these Montreat families is an event separate from the Montreat visiting of summertime, but the visiting here takes on the character of an extended family reunion in itself. One well-known kin group holds its annual reunion at Montreat, using the assembly area at Moore Center near the conference facilities; it follows the classic pattern described for the family reunion throughout the South. The only distinguishing factor is that this particular family has in its past a number of early prominent Presbyterian leaders, ministers, professors, and a college president and is descended from a successful planter who moved to the Piedmont in the early 1800s to become the owner of "the first brick house in the South Carolina upcountry." Clearly a model group of kin, the descendants of this illustrious ancestor today hold numerous posts in the large churches of the denomination, have produced missionaries to China, Korea, Brazil, and Mexico, and have contributed officials to every denominational board and agency. The gathering of this kin group draws 200 people or more. Over 400 known living descendants are specifically recorded in the official history of this family, written by the family's own "local historian" in the manner of a church history. Another family held its 1970 reunion in the Assembly Inn, where over 100 descendants gathered to honor an ancestor who had started a farm in Virginia in the 1790s and whose children migrated to the area, where the Stone Church of Oconee County was founded by "associated families from Virginia." In both these cases the descendants of the common ancestor were holders of prestigious positions in the denominational life and were among the "first missionaries to the Congo" or holders of some other similar distinctions. Also, in both these cases the old family homeplace had been sold many years earlier and, because of having so many ministers and missionaries in the family, there was no one locality except Montreat that the entire group could practically call "home."

The reunion theme is one that runs deep in the life of the Montreat community. Cousins cluster on porches, eating home-made ice cream, sharing stories, talking about childhood, and enjoying seeing one another again. Returned travelers from overseas and missionaries on furlough return to Montreat to reunite with their parents, children, and childhood friends. Conference goers enthusiastically embrace college classmates and friends from former churches whose paths have taken them in separate directions. Collegiate workers return summer after summer to work with the friends they have made through the years and to be near their own parents and cousins who are vacationing in the family's cottage. Reunion of the scattered people is actualized repeatedly over the summer, the scattered "people of God" reassembling again and again to reweave their webs of kinship, friendship, and shared understandings. It is a family reunion but much more. It includes the symbolism and social characteristics of the family reunion and also of the reunion in the church graveyard and in the country cemetery; it carries the cultural themes of the camp meeting and the Chautauqua, adding formalized spiritual renewal and instruction to the familial, genealogical threads. It establishes a pilgrim shrine that is permanent and institutionalized for the representation of the symbols of the Protestant, Presbyterian world.

PART THREE

Meanings

CHAPTER SIX

Symbols, Meanings, and Social Form

The reunion in the rural setting calls on a number of powerful traditional Christian images to portray symbolically the meanings associated with *family*, *home*, and *community* and the contradictions of meanings, the irreconcilable paradoxes, within the religio-familial system of Protestant culture. The family gathered at the reunion has the same social shape and many aspects of the form of liturgy seen in the religious gathering of people for the church homecoming or camp meeting; often one finds the reunion is held at the campgrounds or outdoors around the covered tables near the graveyard of the rural church. The Biblical images of *household of God* and *family of faith* are invoked to sacralize the human family by linking it to the ongoing unit of the church; the image of the *communion of the saints* as a collected body of heavenly and earthly Christians is linked with the specific human ancestors of a family through honor of the old and of the dead and through the tie of reunions to ancient family homeplaces and cemeteries. Sharing common food invokes the image of Holy Communion—in this case consisting of food prepared by the women of each family in the fashion of an offering consumed by all in the sacramental setting of the common table. Finally, the imagery of the Virgin Mary, the Holy Mother, is re-created in Protestant form in the person of the mother of the human family, who is at once a servant and an

127

ethereal being; a procreator of children and a generator of cultural continuity; who is close to the earth, to nature, and to "intuition," yet removed by respect and reverence from the world of the men's domain.

My task here is an ethnographic task, one of drawing together a broad body of material on certain cultural phenomena that give every evidence of being related thematically, historically, and behaviorally, and attempting to understand this class of phenomena—to find out, in other words, just what all the fuss is about regarding reunions and homecomings. In this methodology I have followed Geertz, who admonishes the ethnographer not to construct great overarching laws of the universe from the manipulation of "discovered facts." Instead, he says that "cultural analysis is (or should be) guessing at meanings, assessing the guesses, and drawing explanatory conclusions from the better guesses, not discovering the Continent of Meaning and mapping out its bodiless landscape." About theory he goes on to say that "in ethnography the office of theory is to provide a vocabulary in which what symbolic action has to say about itself—that is, about the role of culture in human life—can be expressed" (Geertz 1973:18).

Reunion Rituals as Text

I have approached the social form of the kin-religious gathering as a text that I have attempted to read in order to learn about the way in which the people of this cultural universe see and write about themselves on the tablet of human social life. One of the clearest explications of this approach is, in my view, Geertz's explication of the use of text as a means of understanding the Balinese cockfight.

> In the case at hand, to treat the cockfight as a text is to bring out a feature of it (in my opinion, the central feature of it) that treating it as a rite or pastime, the two most obvious alternatives, would tend to obscure: its use of emotion for cognitive ends. What the cockfight says it says in a vocabulary of sentiment—the thrill of risk, the despair of loss, the pleasure of triumph. Yet what it says is not merely that risk is exciting, loss depressing, or triumph gratifying, banal tautologies of affect, but that it is of these emotions, thus exampled, that society is built and individuals are put together. Attending cockfights and participating in

them is, for the Balinese, a kind of sentimental education. What he learns there is what his culture's ethos and his private sensibility (or, anyway, certain aspects of them) look like when spelled out externally in a collective text; . . .   (Geertz 1973:449)

I have used this approach to kin-religious gatherings; I have seen the informal outdoor liturgical tradition—the folk liturgy—as a text for analysis. The gatherings are cultural statements, enactments of ethos, of "private sensibilities," of world view and belief turned into concrete social action, symbolizing in pattern, movement, narrative style, and dramatic structure, with its internal behaviors and material artifacts, the meanings associated with the Protestant world, specifically here the world of the Puritan Calvinistic Reformed tradition, and that world's inescapable contradictions. If the cockfight is set apart from the ordinary course of life, as Geertz would have it, lifted "from the realm of everyday practical affairs," and surrounded with "an aura of enlarged importance" (Geertz 1973:448), so are the gatherings I have described. The functionalist might submit that these gatherings, like Geertz's cockfight, serve merely to reinforce aspects of the already existing social order or to alleviate anxieties and insecurities resulting from that order (i.e., kinship ties and religious affiliation here, as would be seen to be true of status discriminations in the functional analysis of the cockfight). Geertz says this is not what sets the cockfight apart and gives it its enlarged importance. He says that it is set apart because, in the case of the cockfight,

it provides a metasocial commentary upon the whole matter of assorting human beings into fixed hierarchical ranks and then organizing the major part of collective existence around that assortment. Its function, if you want to call it that, is interpretive: it is a Balinese reading of Balinese experience, a story they tell themselves about themselves.
(Geertz 1973:448)

I would say that the kin-religious gatherings I have described here provide, in the same manner, a metasocial commentary on postindustrial Protestant culture—the matter of the individual who is at once a part of a human family and of a family of faith caught in the imperative to separate oneself from this human family for purposes of achievement and accomplishment; the matter of assorting female and male into separate cultural universes and then organizing much of religious and secular life around that assortment; the matter of the closed world of the Presbyterian Protestant community against the open world of mobile urban society. The commentary makes use of the basic symbols, images, and metaphors of Protestant Christianity in the movement of the Eucharist out of the central part of the church and onto the altar of the concrete table under the shade of the trees; the movement of the holy family of Mary, her son, her father, from the heavenly church to the worldly one embodied in the family of the human community; the movement of the saints from their communion and intercession in the world of glory into the communion of saints around the tables and in the adjoining graveyards in the unqualified sainthood of those who have been saved by grace and justified by faith. The gatherings are indeed a Protestant reading of Protestant experience.

The requirements of blood, soil, and mind, of walking in the ways of the ancestors that comes from the culture of the *gemeindeschaft* are seen in stark relief against the requirements of individualized salvation, of walking in the part of the pilgrim in individualized industrial society in the ways of the urban world.

Geertz points to Northrup Frye's statement about the play *Macbeth*, to which we go in order "to learn what a man feels like after he has gained a kingdom and lost his soul" (Frye 1964:63-64, quoted in Geertz 1973:450). Geertz calls these kinds of events "paradigmatic human events." The gathering of kin and cobelievers in the events I have described enables the participant, usually isolated from an extended kin group, to learn what it is like to be in a large family where everyone loves and cares for everyone else, where the old are revered, and where four generations share stories and histories; in a church assembly where there are no politics or doctrinal battles and where the community is coresidential and protective. In contrast stand the everyday world of two-generational family nucleation and fragmentation and the everyday world of church schisms and doctrinal and social cleavages or, for some, the everyday loneliness of having no church roots, or worse, no coherent systems of religious beliefs at all.

The experience of *communitas* engendered in the antistructure of the gatherings, the institutionalized *liminality*, is the social milieu in which these cultural messages, these encodements of ethos and world view, can find recurrent expression in social form.

In referring to Geertz's treatment of the cockfight as a paradigmatic event and comparing its significance to the rituals of reunion in the Southeastern United States, I do not imply that these events are in any way connected. They are similar because they hold a similar structural position in the two societies of which they are a part. These events and others like them frame important cultural commentaries on their respective societies and, as such, become examples of what Geertz calls "paradigmatic human events." Far from providing an escape or merely a respite from what is really going on in daily life, these types of events state symbolically some significant aspects of the underlying meanings in the daily life itself. Whereas one thing Geertz says is really going on in all the daily composure and aloofness of Balinese culture is status conflict, I assert that an important element in what is really going on in the isolated, individualistic life-as-pilgrimage model of Protestant experience is the perpetuation of the idea of community and the creation and continuity of extended kin groups and networks. The symbolic expressions in ritual, then, are not simply escapes *from* daily life into fantasy worlds but significant signs of the daily world's inner meanings. Furthermore, these symbolic statements provide a reservoir of cultural materials out of which people draw in order to maintain and transform their worlds.

The family gathering is not, then, merely a *response to* modernization, reformation, urban industrialism, imperialism, or to the migration from Northern Europe and the settling of the American frontier. The gatherings are, in fact, one cultural statement of a Northern European people whose cultural preoccupations led them also to originate and carry out the forceful social developments that shook the Western world.[1] In commenting on the depth and power of these cultural preoccupations of Protestants, Walter Herbert made the following statement as part of his reaction to my description of the reunion of the Worthy family set forth earlier.

> People who are appalled by the wrenching stresses of modern life should shake in their boots when they contemplate the Worthy family getting together in a North Georgia churchyard, because it is exactly people like this who sustain those stresses and have produced the society that imposes them on those who have other traditions.
>   (Herbert 1985, personal communication)

The gatherings I have described are certainly not the only cultural texts commenting on Protestant social form and experience, just as the cockfight is not the only cultural text commenting on that of the Balinese. In Protestant America there are other cultural texts commenting on the world of Protestant Christianity in a multitude of ways, including the Sunday morning worship service, the church family night supper, the youth program, local festivals, bazaars, age-graded and sex-segregated clubs and classes such as Sunday School and the women's and men's associations, complexes of revivals and series of special preaching seasons, festivals of Christmas, Lent, Easter, and many more. To quote Geertz again, "The culture of a people is an ensemble of Texts, themselves ensembles which the anthropologist strains to read over the shoulders of those to whom they properly belong" (Geertz 1973:452).

Reunion and Symbolic Inversion

In attempting to understand the inversion of the Roman Catholic world presented within the symbolic statement of the reunions and homecomings of Protestant culture, one finds an intriguing example of a play upon a play—that is, a symbolic inversion of the pilgrimage process of one existing religious-cultural system through an opposite and contrastive form of social action in the pilgrimage of another religious-cultural system in the same Western society. At the same time the process of pilgrimage itself remains a liminal phenomenon, forming a commentary on and a social complement to each of the particular secular societies within which it finds its place. In other words, in the tight-knit world of the town and burgh, the peasant village, the traditional social structure of the family and kin that Mary Douglas (1973) calls "group-like" social systems, the individual pilgrimage frames a liminal phase of religious life—on the margins, in the transitions, within poverty, and in search of expiation for one's sins. It offers an antisystem that is individualistic in nature. In the individualized world, meanwhile, of the Protestant personal pilgrim whose life is a struggle toward fulfillment and achievement, who is compelled to separate from family, kin, and local community in order to attain success, whose every move is an act of evidence that he or she is among the elect, and whose very occupation or profession is seen as a personal "calling," the pilgrimage of reunions and homecomings becomes the symbolic statement of a world of antisystem that is focused not on the individual but on blood, soil, and mind. The idealized Protestant version of community is unattainable within the structures of the capitalistic urban world of the modern society. The idealized Roman Catholic version of individuality and personhood in the presence of saints and of God is also unattainable in the everyday obligations of the medieval church and society or the Mediterranean, Hispanic-Mexican, and rural Irish cultures within which contemporary Roman Catholic pilgrimages are most popular.

Each pilgrimage, the Roman Catholic and the Protestant, as social form provides a commentary on its own world and in some aspects an inversion of that world, as in the case of ritual liminality of all types. At the same time each pilgrimage provides a commentary on and an inversion of the other pilgrimage—the entire universe of social action and of cosmology being radically different in Roman Catholic and in Protestant pilgrimage as in life and thought. Each fits and reacts and comments on its own structured world while at the same time being symbolically a commentary on the other.

I have written the preceding paragraphs as if these two forms of symbolic action grew up side by side, in historical contemporaneity, which, of course, we know did not happen. Because the pilgrimage of Roman Catholicism is an ancient form going back to the first 100 years after the life of Jesus and finding its most elaborate florescence in the Middle Ages, it is, of course, the form to which the Reformers were forced to react. The Roman Catholic version of pilgrimage calls on the symbolic inventory of the Mediterranean cultural world.

Protestant pilgrimage calls on the symbolic inventory of the Northern European Reformers. The Reformation tradition negated all pilgrimages and focused instead on the life of the person, in actuality reflecting the world view of capitalism and industrialism, of those who wished to see their lives as instruments of individual achievement. The images of the individual leaving home to wander, the solitary person seeking his or her fortune, and the

nuclear and stem families are all deeply rooted in the cultural
tradition of Celtic and Saxon Northern Europe and Britain. The
beliefs of the Calvinists and the Reformers reflect these cultural
images. The English Puritans who eventually settled New England
in the United States and the Scots Presbyterians who settled Ulster
and then the American Southern and Western frontier were especially fervent in these basic Calvinistic Reformation beliefs. The
Roman Catholic and the Protestant forms of pilgrimage, while
representing two different time periods and the ascendancies of two
different European regional cultures (the Mediterranean and the
Northern European-British), might be usefully viewed as also representing two different sides of the same overarching tradition,
which we call Western Christianity.

The concept of ritual inversion as used by anthropologists is a
complex one, used over time in various ways by members of
various intellectual traditions. In attempting to explore this concept
through a collection of essays on the topic, Babcock offers the
following definition.

> "Symbolic inversion" may be broadly defined as any act of expressive
> behavior which inverts, contradicts, abrogates, or in some fashion pre-
> sents an alternative to commonly held cultural codes, values, and norms
> be they linguistic, literary or artistic, religious or social and political. . . .
> Precisely because it is such a widely observed form of symbolic action
> and because the nature of symbols and of expressive behavior has
> become a focus of anthropological concern, symbolic inversion merits
> specific discussion. . . .   (Babcock 1978:14–15)

Symbolic inversion, she goes on to note, is an important aspect of
the liminal phase of ritual. Within liminal phases of ritual, it is
possible to comment on aspects of day-to-day life that are difficult,
contradictory, seemingly unattainable, or disorderly or to rearrange categories so that definitions and meanings conventionally
ascribed to one thing are within the ritual ascribed to another.
These properties of symbolic inversion comment on and question
the social order, but the symbolic commentary may also be a means
of creating and continuing the order itself (Babcock 1978:26–27).

In thinking along these lines, Peacock (1978) reflects on the
interplay between different aspects of the Muslim religious tradition as expressed in the reformist circles in Indonesia such as the

Muhammadijah. The Muhammadijah movement presents an ideology of purification of the faith and of reform of the practices as fervent and as dedicated as that of any Protestant reform group. In the life and thought of the dedicated Muslim puritan the "syncretic" practices of the Javanese theater are abhorrent because they pollute Islam with elements of Hinduism and Buddhism and allow the clown and the transvestite to make playful commentary on life in general, which is offensive because, they say, "Islam is serious." Peacock argues that the theater (the proletarian dramas) and the reformist movements are antithetical to each other because they, in fact, embody two opposing world views. He explains this conflicting ideology and behavior in the following way.

> The symbols of reversal derive their meaning from a classificatory scheme whose categories they serve to connect at any given moment, so as to maintain an eternal, balanced unity. Reform and revolution derive meaning from a linear conception of history that imagines not static divisions but an infinite series of means harnessed to future ends. In Indonesia, the notion is caught in the term *perjuangan*, or struggle, which is central in the ideologies of both Muslims and nationalists and is applied to both the society and the individual. . . .
>
> Conceiving of the life history as a linear process, a struggle, a perdjuangan, reformists and revolutionaries see categories such as male and female, high and lowly, as phases within a sequence rather than fixed divisions within a static structure. They imagine the individual as capable of rising from low to high status within his lifetime, just as Muhammad rose from camel driver to prophet.   (Peacock 1978:220)

Anyone familiar with the pronouncements of the New England Puritans against merriment in general or of the early Calvinists against idols, icons, ritual, processionals, Christmas carols, saints' days celebrations, and other expressions of merriment, revelry, and festivity cannot miss the parallel between Peacock's Muslim puritans and those of the Reformed Protestant tradition. The anti-Catholic and anticlerical sentiment of the rural South is well documented, especially that sentiment and doctrine finding actualization in the summer round of camp meetings and church and cemetery reunions. At Protestant summer outdoor gatherings there are rules against consuming alcohol or drugs, and there is little toleration for public smoking, card playing, or ballroom dancing (although square dancing and reel and circle dancing are sometimes permitted). "Rock" music is not permitted, nor are other secular forms of revelry. There are no plays or dramas, no processionals in the services, and no overt symbols such as banners, icons, stained glass, ministerial vestments, or other religious ecclesiastical paraphernalia. The absence of these elements is a purposeful Protestant reversal of Roman Catholic worship and practice.

The reversals of the social order of daily Protestant life found within Protestant pilgrimage include the subtle but quite real reversals of social position, as in women instead of men as ritual specialists. Old age and infancy are honored categories instead of the secular honoring of the young adult; ancestry and genealogy are the ways of placing persons in the system instead of the lonely individual being classified according to age, sex, and occupation by the mainstream American culture. There are reversals of place—old homeplaces over bright new suburbs, rural over urban, nature over technology—and reversals of time—summertime, weekend time, the Sabbath, over workday routine time with its hourly wage or billable hours. These reversals are, however, couched within the safe context of a legitimized ritual world where the anomalies of the system can be explored and rearranged in ways that do not threaten to destroy the system itself.

Peacock draws a general principle about classificatory world view—that in which positions are fixed and in which those same positions are the subject of fascination in and through dramatic reversals such as those using clowns and transvestites and other forms of rich dramatic imagery. In the argument I put forth about contrasting worlds within Western Christianity, this classificatory world view applies to that of Roman Catholicism. Peacock says the Muslim puritans oppose the dramatic forms of reversal, including clowns and transvestites, because of puritanical uneasiness with symbols that venerate the very cosmic categories whose existence is a threat to the forward struggle of the reform movement. In Peacock's words:

> To state the general principle, drawn from this one case but probably applicable to other cases: the clsasificatory world view, which emphasizes the subsuming of symbols within a frame, nourishes and is nourished by symbols of reversal; the instrumental world view, which emphasizes the sequential harnessing of means to an end, threatens and is threatened by such symbols. The instrumental world view would re-

duce all forms to mere means toward the ultimate end, but symbols of reversal call forth enchantment with the form and veneration of the cosmic categories it embodies, a fixation dangerous to the forward movement, the struggle, the perdjuangan. (Peacock 1978:233)

Further analysis of Peacock's data on the ritual practices within the Muslim reform movement might reveal certain subtle reversals of reform society and practice that would enable a closer comparison between these two parallel social processes—those of Reformed Christianity and of Reformed Islam. The task is one that bears consideration in the future. For the purposes of this commentary, it is sufficient to say that the reversals of the social order that occur within Protestant rituals of reunion do, in fact, overturn accepted categories and also enable the partial resolution of conflicting aspects of day-to-day life. In this sense the rituals do serve, as Babcock (1978) has suggested, all that symbolic inversion serves: to comment on and question the social order, but also to create and continue that same social order itself.

Peacock suggests that the elaborate inversions of the Indonesian theater are congruent with the archaic forms of that society and validate its traditions. He has written in other places of the striking traditional, archaic elements in the society and culture of the Southern United States. It is interesting to note that within this seemingly archaic society there are also strong elements of the ongoing direct reform world view he associates with "modernization," and that even in "modernized" societies one finds examples of symbolic inversions. I would, in light of this complex set of observations, rephrase Peacock's question on how inversions work and what they mean. He asks: "A question hardly considered by anthropological studies of such subjects as symbolic reversal and dualism: how and why are these systems transformed and destroyed by the onslaught of modern society?" (Peacock 1978:233). I would ask instead not only "how and why are these systems transformed and destroyed" but also, "What are the additional, complementary, elaborated or transformed new symbolic systems that emerge during modernization and continue as coexisting systems, side by side with the ones created by earlier cultural traditions and syncretisms?"

Throughout my descriptive and interpretive ethnographic chapters I have presented various aspects of the rituals of reunion in which inversions occur, either of the routines of the secular day-to-day urban world or, in a broader historical, social context, of the world of Roman Catholic pilgrimage. The use of the term *inversion* to express these two seemingly different concepts is not accidental. The first use, the inversion of the routine world in the world of ritual, is a use by anthropologists that appears generally in symbolic anthropology, as in previous passages from Peacock and Babcock. Within the ritual process itself, especially in the liminal phase of ritual, the usual categories recognized by the culture may be rearranged and recombined in various ways in order to restate norms and values or to explore the potential of negation of those norms and values.

The second use of the term *inversion* applies to the wider process of the inversion of the entire Roman Catholic world in the cosmology of Protestantism and to the expression of this inverted universe in the Protestant pilgrimage system. The pilgrimage of Protestantism, I contend, is a pilgrimage complex composed of overlapping networks of people attending the summertime rituals, a return to kin-based cultural worlds entwined with religious rural communities of the idealized past. This form of pilgrimage contrasts sharply with the pilgrimage described by Victor and Edith Turner for Roman Catholic Mediterranean Europe, Ireland, and Mexico and with that of medieval Christianity. And the rural cemeteries, churches, and conference centers contrast sharply with the shrines of the saints and martyrs and with the magical powers associated with these shrines. Both pilgrimages belong to liminality as such, and both rearrange the materials of everyday life into symbolic commentaries on their respective worlds. But also, both pilgrimages express their own separate cultural worlds, one of which—the Protestant—represents an inversion of the other—the Roman Catholic. The entire institutional complex of the Protestant pilgrimage, I contend, states a world view stemming from a root metaphor emerging at the Reformation—a new metaphor that rearranges the materials of the earlier Roman Catholic world and organizes these materials symbolically in radical new ways. In the sense that I present an argument for this position, my work is an attempt to address the complicated question of the relationship between symbolic processes and social change, in this case the relationship between pilgrimage as ritual, as a liminoid phenomenon, and the transformation of society from traditional to modern at the time of the Reformation, including the contemporary expression of those changes.

Function and Meaning in Protestant Ritual

In addressing the questions attending reunion rituals as symbolic statements about Protestant culture and as symbolic inversions of a Roman Catholic pilgrimage complex, one implicitly assumes that these gatherings of kin and coreligionists are serving a social function. At one level, the kin-religious gatherings provide, simply, a means of networking and a device for maintaining continuous ties among kinfolks. They provide at the same time a psychological means of resolving for the participants certain conflicts arising from the need to leave home. A third aspect of the function of the gatherings is that of establishing a code, a language of cultural transmission through which individuals within a particular cultural group can communicate nonverbally, can express to one another through actions their shared meanings and can transmit the culture to the next generation. In contrast to those who have expected the decline in ritual forms with modernity, I submit that this communication aspect of ritual becomes increasingly important as society becomes more complex and individuals within cultures are separated by the forces of modernization. In the individualized milieu of urban society one finds communication in the public sphere to be couched in written documents and formal codes of conduct and verbal rhetoric. In the private sphere, meanwhile, there is more elasticity of behavior and a greater reliance on Bernstein's restricted codes of communication in the stylized and repetitive behavioral forms of family ritual life (Bernstein 1971). Within the setting of kin-religious gatherings in a network of kin and friends whose anxieties and conflicts are temporarily alleviated, this type of nonverbal communicative aspect of ritual takes on enlarged importance. One especially intriguing element of this process is that the people to whom reunions and homecomings are most significant are those who have given intellectual and verbal assent to the principle that ritual is "empty" and "meaningless" and that individual spontaneity is to be preferred in life, thought, and in response to God.

Mary Douglas contrasts those who find meaning in rituals such as the Mass with those who "despise ritual" (whom she would quickly assert are predominantly Protestant or nonreligious but who include also some Roman Catholic laypeople and clergy). She says that these people who "despise ritual" are those who seek to find authenticity through interpersonal communication and social responsibility. She claims, however, that they are deceiving themselves to think that they can live without symbolic expression. In her words:

> The drawing of symbolic lines and boundaries is a way of bringing order into experience. Such non-verbal symbols are capable of creating a structure of meanings in which individuals can relate to one another and realize their own ultimate purposes. . . . Symbolic boundaries are necessary even for the private organizing of experience. But public rituals which perform this function are also necessary to the organizing of society.

She goes on to say:

> These very people, who prefer unstructured intimacy in their social relations, defeat their wish for communication without words. For only a ritual structure makes possible a wordless channel of communication that is not entirely incoherent.   (Douglas 1973:73)

In terms of fulfilling the ritual function of weaving together a network of persons in a scattered Protestant universe, there are, of course, a multitude of varied ritual forms that could be studied. Some of the most obvious of these are the worship services and other activities of congregational life in the weekday/weekend routines of a Protestant church, the rites of passage that attend the individual life cycle—baptism, marriage, funeral service—and the high ceremonial times attending the Christian year at Easter, Thanksgiving, and Christmas that also often elicit "minireunions" of families. In the generalized Protestant culture of Scots and their American descendants there are other ritual gatherings centering on other aspects of life. For various reasons I have limited my attention to those focusing on family and religious themes, those I have identified as "kin-religious" and for the most part rural, annual, and liminal in character.

There are two kinds of events that I have purposely omitted in my treatment of Scottish and American Protestant rituals of reunion that some might nominate on functional grounds for inclusion. These are the gatherings of the Scottish clans in the Highlands and in the United States and the outdoor civic ceremonies of the Scottish Borders (similar, in function if not in form, to the town festivals growing in popularity throughout the Southern and Midwestern United States). I have analyzed these two events elsewhere (Neville 1978). Because they appear on the surface to fit my typology of gatherings reuniting scattered individuals, I will explain my reasons for not including either in the present analysis.

The first type, that of the clan gathering in Scotland and in the United States, is not a family reunion or a religious association, but essentially a secular voluntary association. The clan societies started in this country and for the most part in Scotland in the late nineteenth century.[2] They are in the United States somewhat similar to other genealogy-validating associations such as the Daughters of the American Revolution, the United Daughters of the Confederacy, and the Daughters of the Republic of Texas. They are, however, based not only on proved genealogy for the regular member but on the possession of a particular surname, or of a mother with that surname, identified with a clan family. The clan societies express a fascination with kinship and with heritage that is typical of the colonial Scots and Scotch-Irish around the world. The clans were historically associated with Highland Scotland and with people whose primary ties were not congregational. The Scottish Covenanters and the colonial Presbyterians were associated with the Lowlands and Midlands of Scotland as well as with Ulster, and their close ties of church and community are well known. The clan gatherings certainly could not in any way be classified as "kin-religious gatherings." They are not connected in any explicit formal or symbolic ways with Presbyterianism or with churches. They, in fact, express many feudal, hierarchical, and anti-Protestant themes through their focus on pageantry, military processionals, and games of brute strength and skill and their inclusion of gaiety and revelry that includes heavy drinking and, almost always, dancing. Their primary tradition stems from the military, their identification often is with the rebellion of the clans against the English in 1745 in support of Bonnie Prince Charlie in his claim to the throne. Their favored costume for ceremonial display is that of the tartan and the kilt, copied from military garb. Their only religious moment is usually in the "kirkin' of the tartans" early in any clan gathering, a ceremony resembling closely the traditional "blessing" given by Roman Catholic priests to secular activities of various kinds, including wars and colonial expeditions.

The second type of event, the town festival, is also secular and civic in nature. In civic ceremonial times in Border Scotland foot processionals take to the streets, following the banners of various trade associations and other clubs fashioned on the medieval guilds, while horse processions follow a standard bearer who carries the flag representing the town. In these ceremonies there is often a perambulation of the town's boundaries or of the boundaries of the town's common lands, giving the festival its name of Common Riding or Riding of the Marches. These civic ceremonies, while found in Scotland and outdoors and while serving the social function of reassembling scattered urban people, are a second example of outdoor assemblies *not* a part of the symbolic complex I have described as Protestant pilgrimage. The civic ceremony is the quintessential secular ritual in that it secularizes formerly holy imagery of Roman Catholicism and uses the forms of Roman Catholic liturgy, notably the processional, in a totally desacralized, secular setting to state loyalty not to the mother church but to the mother burgh or town.[3] While the functions of all these events may be similar—that is, to reunite people who have gone away and to serve the purpose of a center for collection of groups who perceive themselves to be related in some way through clan, town, or trade guild—the meanings they convey are totally different. The clan gatherings and the town ceremonies convey meanings that are military and civic in character. These secular, civic events are symbolic commentaries on certain features of the migration outward into the colonial territories, just as the kin-religious gatherings, reunions, and homecomings comment on other aspects of migration of persons and reformation of ideas and beliefs attendant to that migration. Clan gatherings and town ceremonies symbolically construct a different social world for their participants from the symbolic world created and passed along by those serious Protestants who reassemble in honor of their religious heritage, their ancestors' adherence to the Protestant imperative, and their own affiliation with the ongoing covenant community.

Within the framework of pilgrimage and its relation to the society of the medieval church and world and to the church and world of modern Protestantism, I have attempted here to demonstrate the patterns of this particular Protestant symbolic complex and to excavate its layers of meaning. Through understanding the internal processes of reunion and homecoming and placing these events against the backdrop of economic and social history, we may reach a greater depth of understanding of the drama of Protestant experience and of the place of this drama in the life and thought of Western civilization.

Kinship and pilgrimage run side by side as themes of social identity in Western Protestantism, especially that of the United States. Here in the new land shaped by the people whose Old World kinship did not award to them the benefits of inherited land, title, rank, or power, the concept of individual pilgrimage became a root metaphor for the life of free enterprise and personal gain. The pilgrim wanders in order to seek a goal, leaves home, reaches out, accepts the risks and dangers of the journey. In the life-as-pilgrimage motif the person travels alone and is answerable personally to God. Protestant pilgrimage is at one time the individual life journey and the return journey for reunion with others who have also gone out alone. The pilgrimage of reunion is that not only of individuality but also of kinship—the corporate body of the elect, the family of faith, whose founders are honored ancestors and whose descendants are the ongoing people of God.

Notes

Introduction

1. The original fieldwork in Montreat, North Carolina, was done as research for a doctoral dissertation presented in 1971 to the University of Florida Department of Anthropology (See Neville 1971; also Neville 1974). Ethnographic research on reunions and homecomings was conducted in North Georgia between 1971 and 1979 and continued in Texas between 1979 and the time of writing. In the early phases of this work a survey questionnaire was administered to over 300 respondents in approximately equal numbers of Presbyterians, Methodists, and Baptists in Atlanta, Georgia, all of whom had participated in reunions and homecomings. (See Hunnicutt 1974; also see Neville and Hunnicutt 1974.) Fieldwork in Scotland was conducted during the summers of 1972, 1975, 1977, and 1978 (See Neville 1979).

Names of persons and places have generally been changed in order to protect the privacy of the people who so graciously invited me to share in their very private lives and celebrations. The identity of some camp meeting grounds and cemeteries is revealed, as is that of the Presbyterian summer community at Montreat, North Carolina. In the case of Montreat it would be as impossible to disguise the identity of the conference center as it would be to disguise a major European pilgrim shrine. The Baptist conference center at Ridgecrest and the Methodist one at Lake Junaluska, both in North Carolina within a short distance of Montreat, represent similar highly visible and well-known examples of nuclei for Protestant pilgrimage at the transregional level of participation.

144

Chapter One

1. Segments of this chapter were presented at the key symposium of the Southern Anthropological Society and published as "Protestant Pilgrims and Inter-Urban Linkages: the American South and Scotland" in Tom Collins (ed.), *Cities in a Larger Context*. Proceedings of the Annual Meeting of the Southern Anthropological Society. Athens: University of Georgia Press.

2. Some examples of studies by various social scientists, including geographers, sociologists of religion, and urban anthropologists, are those of Gurgel (1976) on Mormon pilgrimage to upstate New York; Birks (1977) and Danbar (1977) on pilgrimages to Mecca; Tanaka (1977) on pilgrimage in Japan; Davis (1983) on Japanese pilgrimage in comparative perspective; and Moore (1980) on secular pilgrimage in the United States to Walt Disney World and other symbolic secular centers. The literature on pilgrimage is extensive, and it is growing. Many studies point out that the process is liminal in nature, or marginal and symbolic to the society in which it exists.

3. In addition to the many general histories of medieval Christianity, see the following for specific studies of the pilgrimages of the times: Heath (1911), Sumtion (1975), Hall (1965), Jusserand (1950), and Zacher (1976).

4. The earliest pilgrimage centers were in the Middle East, including the shrines of the Holy Land and all their internal locales of sacred activity. Later, visions of the Celtic saints and other Northern European Christians sometimes established local versions of the Holy Land, the scene of Nazareth or Bethlehem, and so forth. In the later Middle Ages and early modern era, visions were often of the Virgin Mary and miracles were performed by her. (See Turner and Turner 1978 for a detailed classification of these types and their accompanying theologies.)

5. The town festival in Southern Scotland is also an important point of assembly for urbanites who are former town dwellers. Because it is not specifically religion or kinship based, however, it is not analyzed here but left for a future book examining civic ceremony in greater detail. For one treatment of the burgh and its ceremonies, see Neville (1979).

6. See Posey (1966) and Bruce (1974) for two different historical approaches to the camp meeting tradition.

Chapter Two

1. An earlier version of this chapter was presented at a symposium entitled "The American South in Cross-Cultural Perspective" organized

by James Peacock for the Annual Meeting of the Southern Anthropological Society, March 1976. Some segments were later published in the article entitled "Outdoor Worship as a Liturgical Form" in Neville and Westerhoff (1978).

2. The celebration of an annual "Communion Season" is reported as late as 1929 in the Hebrides, where today a traditional version of Scottish Presbyterianism continues. See Owen (1977).

3. For documentation on this settlement wave, and on the history of Presbyterians in the Southern United States there are many fine histories. See, for example, Leyburn (1962), Sweet (1964), and Thompson (1963).

4. For a detailed treatment of the camp meeting tradition see Boles (1972), Bruce (1975), Johnson (1955), Posey (1966), and Sweet (1930).

Chapter Three

1. See Schneider (1968) on American kinship analyzed within the cultural framework.

2. For more information on the Scots and Scotch-Irish moving westward in family clusters, see Leyburn (1962) and Owsley (1949). See also, on religion of these settlers, Sweet (1964) and Thompson (1963.

3. The theme of light versus darkness and the theme of civilization versus nature are recurrent themes in nineteenth-century literature and thought. The expression of these themes in social action is explored masterfully in Herbert's study of American encounters with the primitive world in *Marquesan Encounters: Melville and the Meaning of Civilization* (Herbert 1981).

4. Observers of American culture from Tocqueville in the 1830s to Bellah and his associates in 1985 have noted that Americans live suspended between the two poles of individualism and communalism. See Tocqueville (trans. 1969); Bellah et al. (1985).

5. Frese (1982) has studied the symbolic use of food in life crisis rituals, focusing especially on the wedding; see also Crocker's comments on food symbolism in the Southern funeral in Crocker (1971). I have treated neither funerals nor weddings, both of which are significant ritual occasions in the life cycle of the Protestant family, and both of which occasions reflect some of the same themes I have explored in calendrical kin-religious gatherings.

6. See Bowmer (1951) and Goodale (1953) on early fellowship meals in Methodism as an example of the notion of fellowship of the believers as communion.

7. See Bernstein (1971).

Chapter Four

' 1. Halpern and Halpern (1972) report, for instance, that in villages in Yugoslavia it is customary to visit the graves with food and leave portions to be consumed by the deceased. Douglass (1969) reports preoccupation with death and the dead as a central cultural theme in Basque society. Badone (1985) finds that in rural Brittany the annual festival of *Toussaint*, or All Saints' Day, is an important ritual for the villagers who have moved away so that they might return to honor the dead and to reunite with family members.

2. See Brackett (1905).

3. See McGeachy (1954).

4. Personal conversation with Thomas Spence, transcribed from field notes for the study of Montreat, North Carolina, 1970. See also Spence (1954) for a history of the Rocky River congregation.

5. Somerville (1939) is the local historian of the Hopewell Presbyterian Church.

6. The pamphlet published by the Salem Camp Ground Association in 1978 entitled "Salem Camp Ground Annual Meeting: August 11–18, 1978" announces the one hundred and fiftieth anniversary of this campground and provides history, information on lodging, and a list of speakers.

7. These gatherings for the Atlanta area were described by Susan Plunkett in a class project for an Emory University seminar in 1975. See Plunkett (1975); Hill (1982) also describes North Georgia Camp Meetings; see also Rees (1984) for a description of a camp meeting in Southwest Arkansas.

8. Complete historical treatment of camp meetings may be found in the following works: Bruce (1974); Cross (1965); Johnson (1955); Sweet (1945); and Weisberger (1958).

9. See Evans (1959) for participant reporting on the Bloy's Cowboy Camp Meeting.

Chapter Five

1. My study of the Montreat summer community was conducted in the summer of 1970. Although there have been certain organizational changes in the Presbyterian Church over the years, my Montreat informants report that the basic patterns I have reported remain the same. I therefore present this section in the "ethnographic present" in the tradition of social anthropology. For the complete community study, see Neville (1971).

2. Several advertising pamphlets appeared at this time directed at prospective buyers of lots and houses in the developing location. One of these is the pamphlet to which I refer, entitled "Mountain Retreat: March Statement 1898." Another publication, a promotional booklet, is also entitled "Mountain Retreat" and was published in New Haven, Connecticut, in 1898. Both authorships are attributed to John R. Collins (1898a and 1898b) and are found in the archives of the Presbyterian Historical Foundation at Montreat, North Carolina.

3. In Mr. Collins' promotional booklet he notes that the site was suggested by Mr. S. W. Hardwick of Atlanta, who was the general passenger agent with Southern Railroad.

4. See Collins (1898a).

5. Collins (1921). Personal letter to Mr. W. S. Bassett. From the archives in the Presbyterian Historical Foundation, Montreat, North Carolina.

6. During this time period the Belk family of Belk Department Stores donated the first playground; Mrs. C. E. Graham of Greenville, South Carolina, donated a dam for the creek, creating Lake Susan, named for a family member; Mr. W. C. Whitner of Rock Hill, South Carolina, provided free engineering work; Mrs. A. T. McCallum of Red Springs, North Carolina, gave a concrete bridge; and Mrs. L. Richardson of Greensboro, North Carolina, donated the materials for the World Missions Building (Anderson 1948).

7. Some of these same preachers were speakers at Montreat in its early days, including Wilbur Chapman, who built a summer home there. In recent years the well-known evangelist Billy Graham built his own home at Montreat and considers it his permanent residence.

8. Quoted by E. T. Thompson (1963:152) from J. R. Howerton, "Montreat—A Presbyterian Chautauqua" in *The Southern Presbyterian*, March 1, 1906.

9. See Hobsbawm (1983); see also Ranger (1983) and Cannadine (1983).

Chapter Six

1. I am indebted for these insights to T. Walter Herbert, Jr. (personal communication 1985).

2. For a detailed analysis of clans as political entities, see Fox (1974).

3. For a more detailed description and analysis of town festivals in Scotland, see Neville (1986).

References

Anderson, Robert Campbell. 1948. *The Story of Montreat from its Beginning 1897–1947*. Published privately at Montreat, North Carolina.

Arensberg, Conrad M. 1963. "The Old World Peoples: The Place of European Cultures in World Ethnography." *Anthropological Quarterly* 36 (3):75–99.

Arensberg, Conrad M. 1965. *The Irish Countryman*. New York: Natural History Press.

Arensberg, Conrad M., and Solon T. Kimball. 1940. *Family and Community in Ireland*. Cambridge, Mass.: Harvard University Press.

———. 1965. *Culture and Community*. New York: Harcourt, Brace & World, Inc.

Austin American Statesman. "Liberty Hill to Incorporate Cemetery Group." Wednesday, June 10, 1953.

Babcock, Barbara. 1978. "Introduction" in Barbara A. Babcock (ed.). *The Reversible World: Symbolic Inversion in Art and Society*. Ithaca, N.Y.: Cornell University Press.

Badone, Ellen. 1985. "New Meanings for the Festival of the Dean in Rural Brittany." Paper presented at the Annual Meeting of American Anthropological Association. Washington, D.C. December 1985.

Barr, James. 1947. *The Scottish Covenanters*. Glasgow: John Smith and Son.

Baskerville, Charles Read. 1920. "Dramatic Aspects of Medieval Folk Festivals in England." *Studies in Philology* XVII (1):1–66.

Bellah, Robert N., Richard Madsen, William M. Sullivan, Ann Swidler, and Steven M. Tipton. 1985. *Habits of the Heart: Individualism and*

Commitment in American Life. Berkeley: University of California Press.

Bernstein, Basil. 1971. *Class, Codes, and Control: Vol. I. Theoretical Studies Towards a Sociology of Language*. London: Routledge and Kegan Paul, Ltd.

Birks, J. S. 1977. "Overland Pilgrimage from West Africa to Mecca: Anachronism or Fashion?" *Geography* 62:215–217.

Black, William. 1975. Unpublished manuscript collected as fieldwork in the seminar on Cultures of the American South, Emory University.

Black, Max. 1962. *Models and Metaphors: Studies in Language and Philosophy*. Ithaca, N.Y.: Cornell University Press.

Boles, John B. 1972. *The Great Revival, 1787–1805: The Origins of the Southern Evangelical Mind*. Lexington: University Press of Kentucky.

Boon, James. 1973. "Further Operations of Culture in Anthropology: A Synthesis of and for Debate" in Louis Schneider and Charles Bonjean (eds.), *The Idea of Culture in the Social Sciences*. Cambridge, England: Cambridge University Press.

———. 1982. *Other Tribes, Other Scribes*. Cambridge, England: Cambridge University Press.

Bordieu, Pierre. 1973. "The Berber House" in Mary Douglas (ed.), *Rules and Meanings*. Hammondsworth, Middlesex: Penguin Books.

Bowmer, John C. 1951. *The Sacrament of the Lord's Supper in Early Methodism*. London: Dacre Press, Adam and Charles Black, Ltd.

Brackett, Richard Newman (ed.). 1905. *The Old Stone Church, Oconee County, South Carolina*. Published privately at Oconee, South Carolina: The Old Stone Church and Cemetery Association.

Bruce, Dickenson D., Jr. 1974. *And They All Sang Hallelujah: Plain-Folk Camp-Meeting Religion, 1800–1845*. Knoxville: University of Tennessee Press.

Brown, Harriet Conner. 1929. *Grandmother Brown's Hundred Years 1827–1927*. Boston: Little, Brown and Company.

Brown, J. G. 1960. *Religious Life in Southwest Scotland Since 1560*. Castle Douglas, Scotland: Broughton House Exhibition.

Burns, Robert. 1795. (Pub. 1909) "The Holy Fair" in Charles W. Eliot (ed.), *The Poems and Songs of Robert Burns*. Volume 6 of The Harvard Classics. New York: P. F. Collier & Son.

Cannadine, David. 1983. "The Context, Performance and Meaning of Ritual: The British Monarchy and the 'Invention of Tradition,' c. 1820–1977" in Eric Hobsbawm and Terence Ranger (eds.), *The Invention of Tradition*. Cambridge, England: Cambridge University Press, pp. 43–100.

Chadwick, Nora. 1963. *Celtic Britain*. London: Thames and Hudson.

Chapman, Malcolm. 1978. *The Gaelic Vision in Scottish Culture*. London and Montreal: Croom Helm and McGill-Queens University Press.

Collins, John R. 1898a. "Mountain Retreat: March Statement 1898." Pamphlet.

———. 1898b. *Mountain Retreat*. Published privately at New Haven, Connecticut.

———. 1921. Personal letter to M. W. S. Bassett. Archives of the Presbyterian Historical Foundation, Montreat, North Carolina.

Crocker, Christopher, 1971. "The Southern Way of Death" in J. K. Morland (ed.), *The Not So Solid South*. Athens: The University of Georgia Press, pp. 114–129.

Cross, Whitney R. 1965. *The Burned-Over District: The Social and Intellectual History of Enthusiastic Religion in Western New York, 1800–1850*. New York: Harper & Row, Publishers.

Danbar, G. S. 1977. "West African Pilgrims to Mecca." *Geographic Review* 67:483–484.

Davis, Winston. 1983. "Pilgrimage and World Renewal: A Study of Religion and Social Values in Tokugawa, Japan, Part I." *History of Religions* 23(2):97–116.

———. 1984. "Pilgrimage and World Renewal: A Study of Religion and Social Values in Tokugawa, Japan, Part II." *History of Religions* 23(3):197–221.

Dickson, R. J. 1966. *Ulster Emigration to Colonial America*. London: Routledge and Kegan Paul, Ltd.

Dix, Dom Gregory. 1945. *The Shape of the Liturgy*. London: Dacre Press, Adams and Charles Black, Ltd.

Douglas, Mary. 1973. *Natural Symbols*. New York: Random House Vintage Books.

Douglass, William A. 1969. *Death in Murelaga*. Seattle: University of Washington Press.

Dowse, Ivor. 1964. *Pilgrim Shrines of Scotland*. London: The Faith Press.

Edminston, Douglas C. 1974. "Communion Tokens" in *Scottish Field*. April 1974. Reproduced for a museum exhibit in Kirkudbright, Scotland: The Stewartry Museum.

Evans, Joe M. 1959. *Bloys Cowboy Camp Meeting*. El Paso, Texas: Guynes Publishing Co.

Feeley-Harnick, Gillian. 1981. *The Lord's Table: Eucharist and Passover in Early Christianity*. Philadelphia: University of Pennsylvania Press.

Firth, Raymond. 1973. *Symbols: Public and Private*. Ithaca, N.Y.: Cornell University Press.

Fortes, Meyer. 1966. "Totem and Taboo." *Proceedings of the Royal Anthropological Institute* 5(22).

Fox, Richard. 1974. "Lineage Cells and Regional Definition in Complex

Societies" in Carol Smith (ed.), *Regional Analyses Vol. II Social Systems*. New York: Academic Press.

Fox, Robin. 1967. *Kinship and Marriage*. Hammondsworth, Middlesex: Penguin Books.

Frese, Pamela R. 1982. *Holy Matrimony: A Symbolic Analysis of American Wedding Ritual*. PhD dissertation, Department of Anthropology, University of Virginia.

Frye, Northrup. 1964. *The Educated Imagination*. Bloomington: University of Indiana Press.

Geertz, Clifford. 1973. *The Interpretation of Cultures*. New York: Basic Books Inc./Harper Colophon Books.

Goodlae, Robert W. 1953. *The Sacraments in Methodism*. Nashville: The Methodist Publishing House.

Gurgel, K. D. 1976. "Travel Patterns of Canadian Visitors to the Mormon Culture Hearth." *Canadian Geography* 20:205–418.

Hall, Donald. 1965. *English Medieval Pilgrimage*. London: Routledge and Kegan Paul, Ltd.

Hall, E. T. 1966. *The Silent Language*. Garden City, N.Y.: Doubleday & Company, Inc.

Halpern, Joel M., and Barbara Kerewsky Halpern. 1972. *A Serbian Village in Historical Perspective*. New York: Holt, Rhinehart and Winston.

Hanson, F. A. 1975. *Meaning in Culture*. London: Routledge and Kegan Paul, Ltd.

Heath, Sidney Herbert. 1911. *Pilgrim Life in the Middle Ages*. London: T. F. Unwin.

Herbert, T. Walter, Jr. 1981. *Marquesan Encounters: Melville and the Meaning of Civilization*. Cambridge, Mass.: Harvard University Press.

———. 1985. Letter to the Author. June 1985.

Hill, Carole E. 1982. "The Meaning of the Religious Campmeeting Experience in the American South." *Anthropology and Humanism Quarterly* 7(2 & 3):39–44.

Hunnicutt, Jack G. 1974. "Kin-Religious Gatherings in the American South." Unpublished Master's thesis. Department of Sociology, Emory University.

Hobsbawm, Eric. 1959. *Primitive Rebels*. New York: W. W. Norton & Company, Inc.

———. 1983. "Mass-Producing Traditions: Europe 1870–1914" in Eric Hobsbawm and Terence Ranger (eds.), *The Invention of Tradition*. Cambridge, England: Cambridge University Press, pp. 263–308.

Johnson, Charles A. 1955. *The Frontier Camp Meeting: Religion's Harvest Time*. Dallas: Southern Methodist University Press.

Jones, Yvonne. 1980. "Kinship Affiliation Through Time: Black Homecomings and Family Reunions in a North Carolina County." *Ethnohistory* 27(1):49–66.

Jordan, Terry. 1982. *Texas Graveyards*. Austin: University of Texas Press.

Jusserand, Jean Adrien. 1950. *English Wayfaring Life in the Middle Ages*. New York: G. P. Putnam's Sons.

Kimball, Solon T., and James E. McClellan, Jr. 1962. *Education and the New America*. New York: Vantage Books/Random House.

LePlay, Frederic. 1884. *L'organization de la Famille*. Paris: Tours.

Leyburn, James G. 1962. *The Scotch-Irish, A Social History*. Chapel Hill: University of North Carolina Press.

Liberty Hill Cemetery Association, Myreta Matthews, Secretary. 1984. *Liberty Hill Cemetery: A Brief History and Roster of Burials*. Published privately at Liberty Hill, Texas, by the Liberty Hill Cemetery Association.

McGeachy, Neill R. 1954. *A History of the Sugar Creek Presbyterian Church*. Published privately at Charlotte, North Carolina, by the Sugar Creek Presbyterian Church.

Melton, Julius. 1967. *Presbyterian Worship in America*. Richmond, Va.: John Knox Press.

Meyerhoff, Barbara. 1983. "The Performance of the Past." Lecture given at the Brown Symposium. Southwestern University.

Moore, G. Alexander. 1980. "Walt Disney World: Bounded Ritual Space and the Playful Pilgrimage Center." *Anthropological Quarterly* 53(4):207–218.

Murray, Alice. 1974. "Salem Camp Ground: Old-Time Religion." *The Atlanta Constitution*, Monday, August 12, 1974.

McElroy, J. 1971. *Seven Kirks in the Stewartry*. Castle Douglas, Scotland: J. McElroy.

Neville, Gwen Kennedy. 1971. "Annual Assemblages as Related to the Persistence of Cultural Patterns: An Anthropological Study of a Summer Community." PhD dissertation, Department of Anthropology, University of Florida.

———. 1974. "Kinfolks and the Covenant: Ethnic Community Among Southern Presbyterians" in John Bennett (ed.), *The New Ethnicity: Perspectives from Ethnology*. Proceedings of the Annual Spring Meeting, American Ethnological Society. Chicago: West Publishing Co.

———. 1978. "Outdoor Worship as a Liturgical Form" in Gwen Kennedy Neville and John H. Westerhoff, III. *Learning Through Liturgy*. New York: Seabury Press.

———. 1979. "Community Form and Ceremonial Life in Three Regions of Scotland." *American Ethnologist* 6(1):93–109.

———. 1980. "Protestant Pilgrims and Inter-Urban Linkages: The American South and Scotland" in Thomas Collins (ed.), *Cities in a Larger Context*. Proceedings of the Annual Spring Meeting of the Southern Anthropological Society. Athens: University of Georgia Press.

———. 1983. "Solon Kimball and the Natural History Method." *Florida Journal of Anthropology* 9:1.

———. 1984. "Learning Culture Through Ritual: The Family Reunion." *Anthropology and Education Quarterly* 15:2.

———. 1986. "Civic Ceremony as Performance, Ritual, and Play: Common Riding in the Scottish Borders." Paper presented to the 85th Annual Meeting of the American Anthropological Association, Philadelphia, December 1986.

Neville, Gwen Kennedy, and Jack G. Hunnicutt, Jr. 1974. "Family and Community in the American South: Recurrent Gatherings and Cultural Transmission." Paper presented to the Annual Meeting of the American Anthropological Society, Mexico City, November 1974.

Newman, P. L. 1965. *Knowing the Gururumba*. New York: Holt, Rhinehart and Winston, Inc.

Nisbet, Robert. 1969. *Social Change and History*. London: Oxford University Press.

Owen, Trefor. 1956. "The 'Communion Season' and Presbyterianism in a Hebridean Community." *Gwerin* I (2):53–66.

Owsley, Frank Lawrence. 1949. *Plain Folk of the Old South*. Baton Rouge: Louisiana State University Press.

Peacock, James. 1968. *Rites of Modernization: Symbolic and Social Aspects of Indonesian Proletarian Drama*. Chicago: University of Chicago Press.

———. 1975. *Consciousness and Change*. New York: John Wiley & Sons.

———. 1978. "Symbolic Reversal and Social History: Transvestites and Clowns of Java" in Barbara Babcock (ed.), *The Reversible World*. Ithaca, N.Y.: Cornell University Press.

Pepper, Stephen. 1942. *World Hypotheses*. Berkeley: University of California Press.

Plant, R. 1974. *Community and Ideology*. London: Routledge and Kegan Paul, Ltd.

Plunkett, Susan. 1975. "Campmeetings Around the Atlanta Area." Unpublished paper prepared for the seminar on Cultures of the American South. Emory University.

Posey, Walter Brownlow. 1966. *Frontier Mission: A History of Religion West of the Southern Appalachians to 1861*. Lexington: University of Kentucky Press.

Ranger, Terence. 1983. "The Invention of Tradition in Colonial Africa" in Eric Hobsbawm and Terence Ranger (eds.), *The Invention of*

Tradition. Cambridge, England: Cambridge University Press, pp. 211–262.

Redfield, Robert W. 1941. *The Folk Culture of Yucatan.* Chicago: University of Chicago Press.

Reese, James A. 1984. *Dwelling in Beulah Land: Davidson Camp Meeting, 1884–1984.* Published privately at Clark County, Arkansas, by the Davidson Camp Meeting Centennial Committee.

Richardson, Fay Bryson. 1970. "Liberty Hill Cemetery Dates Back: Some History of the Liberty Hill Cemetery." *Williamson County Sun,* Georgetown, Texas, November 12, 1970.

Robertson, John F. 1963. *The Story of Galloway.* Castle Douglas, Scotland: William Blackwood and Sons. '

Russell, James. *Reminscences of Yarrow.* Edinburgh: William Blackwood and Sons.

Ryan, Bill. 1980. "Ocean Grove: The Town That Made Time Stand Still." *Parade,* June 1, 1980, pp. 4–5.

Salem Camp Ground Association. 1978. "Salem Camp Ground Annual Meeting: August 11–18, 1978." Pamphlet published privately at Covington, Georgia. by the Salem Camp Ground Association.

Schneider, David. 1968. *American Kinship: A Cultural Account.* Englewood Cliffs, N.J.: Prentice-Hall, Inc.

———. 1976. "Notes Toward a Theory of Culture" in Keith Basso and Henry Selby (eds.), *Meaning in Anthropology.* Albuquerque: University of New Mexico Press, pp. 197–220.

Singer, Milton. 1984. *Man's Glassy Essence: Explorations in Semiotic Anthropology.* Bloomington: Indiana University Press.

Smout, T. C. 1969. *A History of the Scottish People 1560–1830.* London: William Collins Sons & Co., Ltd. (Fontana Paperback Edition 1972).

Sommerville, Charles. 1939. *History of Hopewell Presbyterian Church.* Charlotte, N.C.: The Observer Publishing Co.

Spence, Thomas. 1954. *The Presbyterian Congregation on Rocky River.* Kingsport, Tenn.: Kingsport Press.

Sumption, Jonathan. 1975. *Pilgrimage: An Image of Medieval Religion.* London: Faber and Faber, Ltd.

Sweet, William Warren. 1930. *The Story of Religion in America.* New York: Harper & Bros.

———. 1945. *Revivalism in America, Its Origin, Growth and Decline.* New York: Charles Scribner's Sons.

———. 1964. *Religion on the American Frontier: Vol. I. The Presbyterians.* New York: Cooper Square Publishers, Inc.

Tait, James. 1889. *Two Centuries of Border Church Life.* Kelso, Scotland: J. J. Rutherford.

Tanaka, H. 1977. "Geographic Expression of Buddhist Pilgrim Places on Shikoku Island." *Canadian Geography* 21:111-132.

Thompson, E. T. 1963a. *Presbyterians in the South, Vol. I: 1607-1861.* Richmond, Va.: John Knox Press.

———. 1963b. *Presbyterians in the South Vol. III 1890-1972.* Richmond, Va.: John Knox Press.

Tocqueville, Alexis de. 1969. *Democracy in America,* trans. George Lawrence, ed. J. P. Mayer. New York: Doubleday Anchor Books.

Tönnies, Ferdinan. 1957. *Community and Society,* trans. and ed. Charles A. Loomis. East Lansing, Mich.: Michigan State University Press. (Originally published in 1887.)

Turner, Victor. 1969. *The Ritual Process.* Chicago: Aldine Publishing Company.

———. 1974. *Dramas, Fields, and Metaphors: Symbolic Action in Human Society.* Ithaca, N.Y.: Cornell University Press.

———. 1975. "Death and the Dead in the Pilgrimage Process" in Michael G. Whisson and Martin West (eds.), *Religion and Social Change in Southern Africa.* Capetown: David Philip, pp. 107-127.

Turner, Victor, and Edith Turner. 1978. *Image and Pilgrimage in Christian Culture.* New York: Columbia University Press.

van Gennep, Arnold. 1909. *Les Rites de Passage.* Paris: Emile Nourry.

Vernon, J. J. 1900. "The Parish and Kirk of Hawick 1711-1725." *The Hawick Express Reprint Series.* Hawick, Scotland: The Hawick Express.

Warner, W. Lloyd. 1961. *The Family of God: A Symbolic Study of Christian Life in America.* New Haven, Conn.: Yale University Press.

Weber, Max. 1905. *Die protestaantische Ethik und der Geist des Kapitalismus* translated 1930 by Talcott Parsons. Published in 1958 as *The Protestant Ethic and The Spirit of Capitalism.* New York: Charles Scribner's Sons.

Weisberger, Bernard A. 1958. *They Gathered at the River: The Story of the Great Revivalists and Their Impact on Religion in America.* Boston and Toronto: Little, Brown and Company.

Wilson, Charles Reagan. 1985. "Cemeteries" in Samuel S. Hill (ed.), *Encyclopedia of Religion in the South.* Macon, Ga.: Mercer University Press, pp. 142-143.

Zacher, Christian. 1976. *Curiosity and Pilgrimage: The Literature of Discovery in Fourteenth Century England.* Baltimore: Johns Hopkins University Press.

Index

157

Printed in the United States
35835LVS00002B/91-96